PERFORMANCE-BASED LEARNING AND ASSESSMENT IN MIDDLE SCHOOL SCIENCE

K. Michael Hibbard, Ph.D.

EYE ON EDUCATION
6 DEPOT WAY WEST, SUITE 106
LARCHMONT, NY 10538
(914) 833–0551
(914) 833–0761 fax

Library of Congress Cataloging-in-Publication Data

Hibbard, K. Michael.
    Performance-based learning and assessment in middle school science / K. Michael Hibbard
        p.   cm.
    Includes bibliographical references and indexes.
    ISBN 1-883001-81-1
    1. Science—Study and teaching (Middle school)—United States. 2. Competency based education—
United States.   I. Title.
    Q181.H52   2000
    5507'.1273—dc21   99–40427
                                        CIP

10 9 8 7 6 5 4 3 2 1

Editorial and production services provided by
Richard H. Adin Freelance Editorial Services
52 Oakwood Blvd., Poughkeepsie, NY 12603
(914-471-3566)

Also Available from EYE ON EDUCATION

Personalized Instruction
by James Keefe and John Jenkins

Best Practices from America's Middle Schools
by Charles R. Watson

Collaborative Learning in Middle and Secondary Schools
by Dawn Snodgrass and Mary Bevevino

Writing in the Content Areas
by Amy Benjamin

**Performance Assessment and Standards-Based Curricula:
The Achievement Cycle**
by Allan A. Glatthorn
with Don Bragaw, Karen Dawkins, & John Parker

Performance Standards and Authentic Learning
by Allan A. Glatthorn

A Collection of Performance Tasks and Rubrics
Primary School Mathematics
by Charlotte Danielson and Pia Hansen

Upper Elementary School Mathematics
by Charlotte Danielson

Middle School Mathematics
by Charlotte Danielson

High School Mathematics
by Charlotte Danielson & Elizabeth Marquez

The Performance Assessment Handbook
Vol. 1: Portfolios and Socratic Seminars
Vol. 2: Performances and Exhibitions
by Bil Johnson

The Interdisciplinary Curriculum
by Arthur K. Ellis and Carol J. Stuen

Dedication

This book is dedicated to my wife Beth Wagner
who has helped me to appreciate what is really
worth paying attention to.

ABOUT THE AUTHOR

Dr. K. Michael Hibbard, a former principal and science teacher, is the assistant superintendent for Curriculum, Instruction, Assessment, and Professional Development in the Region 15 Public Schools, which serve the towns of Middlebury and Southbury, Connecticut. He holds a BS in Science from the University of Kansas, a MS in Science from Purdue University, and a PhD in Science Education from Cornell University.

His current work includes writing and professional development in all aspects of standards-based curriculum and assessment. He serves local, national, and international schools. Dr. Hibbard is a contributor to such organizations as the Connecticut State Department of Education, The Connecticut Academy for Education, Project to Increase Mastery in Math and Science, the Association for Supervision and Curriculum Development, Phi Delta Kappan Gabbard Institutes, the National Staff Development Council, the Carnegie Middle School Project, and the Harvard/Annenberg Project in Math and Science.

ACKNOWLEDGMENTS

Special commendations must be given to the administrators and teachers in the Region 15 Public Schools for the work they have done over 10 years to improve student performance in all disciplines including math and science. Region 15 students are now among the top performers at the State and National levels as measured by the Connecticut State tests and the College Board Advance Placement tests.

TABLE OF CONTENTS

1

INTRODUCTION

SIX QUESTIONS TO FOCUS OUR WORK ON IMPROVING STUDENT PERFORMANCE

These six questions provide a framework for the creation and use of assessment, including performance assessment in science:

Question 1: What should students know and be able to do?

This is the question that leads us to develop curriculum standards.

- Chapter 3 and Appendix A of this book.

Question 2: What kinds of tests and performance tasks shall we construct to see how well students perform?

This question leads us to plan a variety of instruments and strategies to collect data on student performance. Tests include the whole range from fact-level multiple choice to long-term research projects. This book focuses on the development of open-ended performance tasks.

- Chapters 2, 5, 7, and 8 and Appendix A.

Question 3: How well should students perform?

This question leads us to the identification of benchmarks or examples of student work that show how well we think students should perform. We can set high goals by the quality of the models we use to define quality work. This question must be answered in your own classroom, school, and school district.

- Touched on in Chapter 6.

Question 4: How well do students actually perform?

This question leads us to make assessment tools, such as rubrics and assessment lists, to describe the strengths and weaknesses of the work students actually do on the tests we give them.

- Chapter 6 and Appendix C.

Question 5: To what degree are we satisfied with the quality of our students' actual performance?

This question asks us to compare the actual quality of student performance to our expectations (high goals) for student performance.

This question is answered in your own classroom through your comparison of your students work and the goals you have set for the performance.

Question 6: What shall we do to improve student performance?

This question asks us to plan improvements in curriculum, instruction, testing, selection of materials, organization of classroom time, and professional development to improve student performance. Work on question 6 is most effective when done in the context of answers to the first five questions. This means that our work to write curriculum and plan instruction should be based on our analysis of the data that comes from a variety of tests and performance assessments of student performance.

This entire book is about improving student performance. Chapter 3 describes how performance tasks are both learning activities embedded in instruction and opportunities to assess student performance. Backward planning described in Chapter 3 shows how a teacher plans day-to-day lessons in response to the performance task(s) that will be used.

- Chapter 3.

A BALANCED APPROACH

While performance assessment is essential to a well-rounded assessment plan, it should not be used exclusively. Traditional testing has an important role to play, particularly in the assessment of a large domain, or in the evaluation of student knowledge. But in assessing how well students can apply their knowledge, some type of performance assessment is essential. Balance is the key word. What follows is a sample grading rationale that shows how the performance task is balanced with the other components of the course to yield an overall grade. Also presented is a plan that shows the balance of the various forms of constructed-response tasks used during the school year in a science class.

SAMPLE GRADING RATIONALE

Component	*Percent of Final Grade*
Tests/Quizzes	20%
Science Lab Book	20%
Class Note Book	10%
Homework	10%
Class Participation	5%
Performance Tasks	35%

THIS BOOK'S FOCUS

This book focuses on the construction and classroom use of performance assessment and the evaluation of student work in response to performance tasks. It contains a collection of performance tasks used in middle school science, along with templates and strategies used by teachers who both utilize and create performance tasks in their own classrooms.

"Performance assessment" means any assessment of student learning that requires the evaluation of student writing, products, or behavior. That is, it includes all assessment except multiple choice, matching, and true/false testing. Classroom-based performance assessment includes all assessment that occurs in the classroom and that is evaluated by teachers, as distinct from, for example, large-scale, statewide performance-testing programs.

Performance assessment is fundamentally criterion-referenced rather than norm-referenced. That is, teachers who adopt performance assessment in science are concerned with the degree to which students can demonstrate knowledge and skill in science and related disciplines, such as math, language arts, and even social studies. Teachers establish the criteria for excellent work "up front" so that teachers, students, and their parents know what is expected. Student work is then measured against these criteria rather than against the work of other students.

Figure 1.1 shows the structure for the chapters 2 through 6 of this book. Chapter 2 presents a performance task, titled *Creature Feature,* along with student work and its assessment. The chapter includes a description of how the task was used and what the teacher learned from her study of student performance. The next four chapters provide background for the development of *Creature Feature.* Chapter 3 explains how performance tasks are embedded in classroom instruction rather than added-on. Chapter 4 addresses Curriculum Standards, chapter 5 outlines a template for making performance tasks, and chapter 6 presents several different types of scoring tools.

FIGURE 1.1. STRUCTURE OF CHAPTERS 2–6

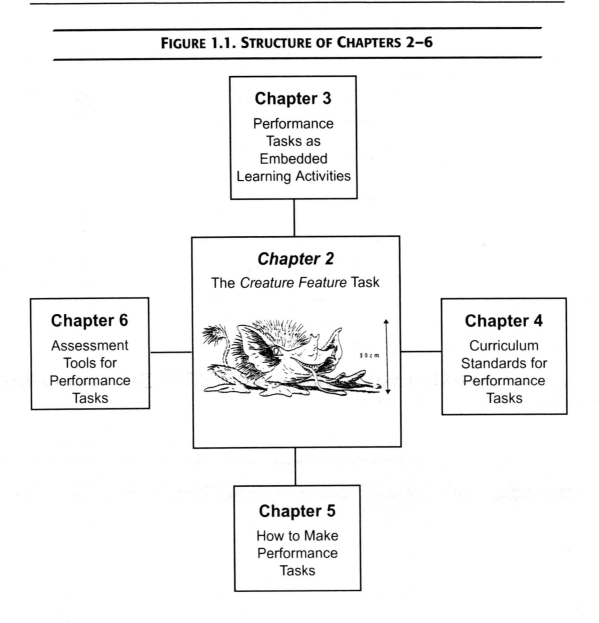

Chapter 7 focuses on a scientific method.

Finally, many examples of performance tasks and support materials are contained in the four appendices: Appendix A is a collection of performance tasks with curriculum standards listed for each task; Appendix B provides some graphic organizers that are useful for science tasks; and Appendix C is a collection of generic frameworks through which to view student work.

OUR ULTIMATE GOAL IS FOR STUDENTS TO BE MOTIVATED, CAPABLE, INDEPENDENT LEARNERS

Figure 1.2 lists the dimensions of what is called "Performance Maturity." These are the characteristics we want our students to develop, and our job is to coach them to be more performance mature when they finish a year with us than they were on the first day of the school. The materials and strategies of performance-based learning and assessment presented in this book help us meet that goal. The strategies of self-assessment and goal setting to improve performance are especially important to developing Performance Maturity.

FIGURE 1.2. PERFORMANCE MATURITY

An Important Goal Is to Improve the Performance Maturity of All Students So That They Will Be Life-Long Learners

Performance maturity is the degree to which an individual works independently to:

- Produce quality work that shows deep understanding of essential concepts within and among disciplines.

- Produce quality work that shows connections between schoolwork and its application to the larger world.

- Use information location, selection, and gathering strategies in appropriate and flexible ways.

- Use problem-solving strategies in appropriate and flexible ways.

- Use productive work habits.*

- Use skills of collaboration.†

- Use a rich repertoire of skills to produce final products in many formats.

- Communicate to a variety of audiences for a variety of specific purposes.†

- Show respect for the personal, intellectual, and property rights of others.*†

- Self-assess and self-evaluate accurately.*

- Make and carry out goals to improve.*

Many of these dimensions of performance maturity include the use of technology as authentic tools for learning.

* = Intrapersonal skills; † = Interpersonal skills

2

THE CREATURE FEATURE PERFORMANCE TASK

Creature Feature, which is shown in Figures 2.1 through 2.3, was created for and used as a two-class period learning and assessment task for a seventh grade Life Science unit called "Structured for Survival."

The performance task in Figure 2.1 (p. 10) has these components:

- The statement of *background* provides a "story line" for the task. It helps make the task interesting to the students.

- The statement of the *task* tells the student what he or she must do.

- The statement of *audience* tells the student the audience for whom the final product is intended. In this case, the final audience is "scientists," which means that technical vocabulary can be used. If the audience was "younger children," then specialized vocabulary could not be used.

- The statement of *purpose* section explains what impact the writing is to have on the target audience.

- Finally, the *procedure* briefly outlines the steps to be taken to complete the task.

The graphic organizer in Figure 2.2 (p. 11) accompanies the performance task. The student uses the graphic framework as a planning step to organize the information and eventually to write the final product. In this task, the graphic organizer is not assessed or graded. In some tasks, the graphic organizer could be the final product, and in other cases, it could be assessed and graded along with the final written product. Appendix C provides a collection of graphic organizer templates.

The assessment list in Figure 2.3 (p. 12) is given to the student at the same time as the performance task. The assessment list shows the student what to pay attention to. The teacher distributed 100 points to emphasize how important each item on the list is. An inspection of the specific items on this list indicates that the student must know the science content related to the life functions

7

of animals and how their body structures enable them to meet those functions within the context of specific environments.

Students use the assessment list before they begin their work, during their work, and for self-assessment just before they turn it in to the teacher. In this case, no peer assessment was done, although that type of assessment is often used.

A sample student response is presented in Figures 2.4A (p. 13) and 2.4B (p. 14). The student did the annotations and underlining. As a part of self-assessment, the teacher had asked the student to pay particular attention to items 2 and 3 on the assessment list. To increase the chances that the student would pay attention, the teacher asked the student to show where each of the five pieces of evidence is in his writing. *E1* shows point of evidence number 1, *E2* shows point of evidence number 2, and so on. The student was also asked to underline the evidence and put parentheses around the explanation given for each piece of evidence. When teachers communicate their expectations clearly to students, and when students pay attention to the assessment lists, they do better.

Figure 2.5 (p.15) is the assessment list showing self-assessment and teacher assessment. The student and the teacher agreed for the most part about the quality of this response. Items number 4 and 6 show some disagreement, which is explained in the teachers comments included later in this chapter.

The teacher gave the student the grade of B+ for this writing. A grade is assigned according to the percentage of the total points earned: 90% and up = A; 80–89% = B; 70–79% = C; 60–69% = D; 59% and below = F. Grading is easy to do with these assessment lists. Assessment gives detailed feedback to the student and teacher, and the grade is for the grade book. Using assessment lists for these two purposes improves performance and assigns grades that are reasonably objective.

The student's reflection about his work on this task is displayed in Figure 2.6 (p. 16). Sometimes the teacher asks the student to write a short reflection on how the student perceives himself or herself as a learner. This examples reveals that this student became more aware of the importance of using simple drawings to help his thinking. He may use this strategy on tasks in science and other subjects even when the tasks do not specifically call for drawings.

The science teacher's comments about student performance are provided in Figure 2.7 (p. 16). The science teacher who used the *Creature Features* task had a personal goal to improve student writing in science. As part of her personal plan for professional development, this teacher did two written analyses of student work during the school year. The first is included here. Her study of student work helped her plan ways to improve teaching that will, in turn, improve student performance.

AN ENRICHMENT FOLLOW-UP FOR CREATURE FEATURE

The *Creature Museum* performance task in Figures 2.8 (p. 21) and 2.9 (p. 23) is an optional enrichment activity for the *Creature Feature* performance task.

THE CONTEXT FOR THE CREATURE MUSEUM TASK

Once the students have completed the *Creature Feature* task, they know two things about the food web in which the creature lives. They know the structure of the creature, and they have defended an inference about the creature's environment. From those two points, the student can scientifically infer the appearance of the plants, the creature's food, and the creature's competitors and enemies.

This task may be used for the whole class, or it could be used as a long-term enrichment activity for very motivated students.

THE CREATURE MUSEUM PERFORMANCE TASK

The performance task (Fig. 2.8, p. 21) has the same outline structure of Background, Task, Audience, Purpose, and Procedure as the *Creature Feature* task. All tasks in this book follow this format. The *Creature Museum* task is organized into several subtasks. The teacher has the option of assigning the whole task or just certain parts of the task if time is limited.

THE ASSESSMENT LISTS FOR CREATURE MUSEUM

Figure 2.9 (p. 23) is a series of assessment lists for this task that correspond to the products for each subsection of the task. It is usually better to have several short assessment lists than one very long one.

Each assessment list represents a checkpoint. The student must receive a score of 80% or better on the product of that subtask to be allowed to continue to the next stage of the project. If the score is lower, then revision is necessary.

SUMMARY

This chapter presents the *Creature Feature* performance task. Student work and assessment tools to describe its quality are included. A narrative by a teacher who used this performance task provides a view of how performance-based learning and assessment influences the science classroom. A follow-up enrichment performance task, *Creature Museum,* is also included.

Chapters 3–6 describe how performance tasks are embedded in instruction, how curriculum standards are used to make tasks valid, how to make performance tasks, and how to make assessment tools for performance tasks.

FIGURE 2.1. CREATURE FEATURE

50 cm

Background

A strange, stuffed creature has just been found in an old crate in the basement of the Museum of Natural History. No notes, labels, or records of any kind have been found to provide any information about where the creature came from or how it ended up in a crate in the basement. A careful inspection has verified that the creature is not a hoax. It is your assignment to study the creature and provide a scientific opinion as to this creature's natural habitat.

Task

Your task is to write a scientific explanation of the type of environment in which you think that this creature lived. You may use drawings to help make you points.

Audience

The audience for your paper is other scientists who work at the Museum and at the University. These scientists will want strong proof for any opinion that you might have.

Purpose

The purpose is for you to use your knowledge of science and writing skills to convince other scientists of your opinion.

Procedure

1. Complete the graphic organizer.

2. Provide support for each of your pieces of evidence.

3. Write your explanation. You may use drawings to help you make your point.

4. Use the assessment list for the Creature Feature.

FIGURE 2.2. CREATURE FEATURE GRAPHIC ORGANIZER

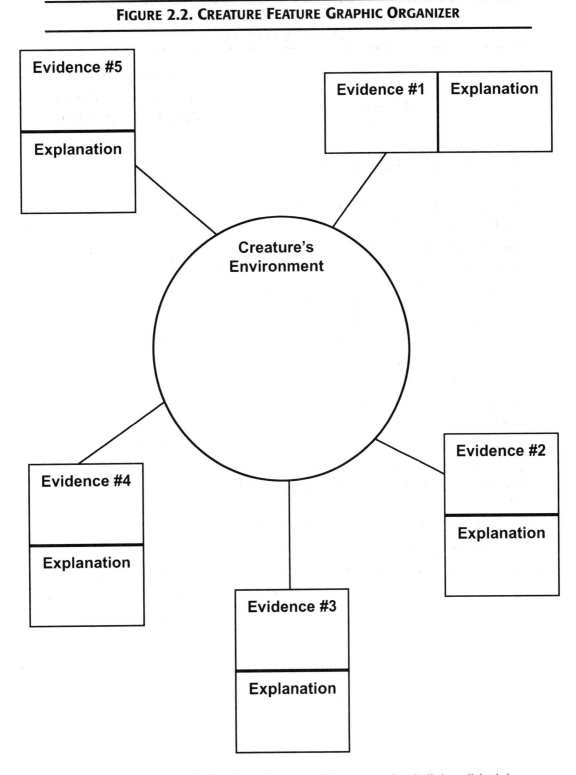

*Note: We have defined environment to mean both living (biotic)
and nonliving (abiotic) elements.*

FIGURE 2.3. PERFORMANCE TASK ASSESSMENT LIST
CREATURE FEATURE

Elements	Points Possible	Earned Assessment Self	Teacher
		Assessment Points	
1. A clear opinion has been stated as to the natural habitat of the creature.	10	____	____
2. At least five pieces of evidence are stated to substantiate the opinion.	20	____	____
3. The relevance and importance of each piece of evidence is explained.	20	____	____
4. An explanation is made as to how all the pieces of evidence "add up" to supporting the identification of the probably natural "home" of the creature.	10	____	____
5. Relevant personal experiences and previous learning is brought in to provide support.	10	____	____
6. Labeled drawings are used to help present the evidence.	5	____	____
7. Scientific words, when used, are explained.	5	____	____
8. The writing, through its vocabulary, examples, and tone, is written as a paper from a scientist to other scientists.	5	____	____
9. The mechanics of English are used correctly.	5	____	____
10. The work is neat and presentable.	5	____	____
11. The work is completed on time.	5	____	____
TOTAL:	100	____	____

FIGURE 2.4A. SAMPLE STUDENT RESPONSE

Fellow Scientists,

I have studied this strange creature which you found in the basement of the museum and I have come to a conclusion that there are two strong possibilities as to the original natural habitat of this mammal. One possibility is that the Creature lived in a wet, marshy environment, but I hypothesize that this creature probably lived in a hot and sandy desert. I will support my hypothesis by describing characteristics of the Creature's morphology that make it well-suited to this desert environment and not as well suited to a marsh. I will also describe the role this organism played in its local food web.

First, I will explain why I think that the creature lives in a hot sandy desert environment. The creature has large, flat, webbed feet which help it to walk on the loose sand without sinking. These feet are similar to the large, flat and soft feet of a camel. Also, large, flat, webbed feet would be a benefit to an animal living in a marsh. The feet alone do not provide strong evidence for whether the Creature lived in a desert or marsh.

However, the ears do provide strong evidence supporting the desert as the natural habitat of this Creature. The large ears help it get rid of extra body heat like the ears of an elephant. In the hot part of the day, this Creature probably held its ears out in a fully extended way to maximize heat loss. At night, when the desert is cold, the ears can be folded in close to the body to minimize heat loss. The big ears would not work for an animal living in the water because they would cause too much resistance as the creature moved through the water or among the reeds and other water pants which would be abundant in a marsh. The ears would continually get caught on the plants and be in the way as the Creature went after food or tried to get away from its predators. Together, the feet and ears support my hypothesis that the desert was the Creature's natural habitat.

FIGURE 2.4B. SAMPLE STUDENT RESPONSE

Now that I have established the desert as the Creature's natural habitat, let me turn my attention to where in the food web this Creature was located. All animals must find food and this creature was probably a secondary consumer eating primary consumers such as mice and insects which in turn eat plants which are the producers. That long nose helped it sniff around among rocks and other hiding places for food. The big eyes are like those of an owl which allow the creature to find its food in dim light in the cool night when small animals and insects become more active. The creature has long hind legs which help it leap at its prey. An animal this large (about the size of my small dog) would probably creep towards small rodents and large insects it hear scurrying around over the sand at night and then leap at them and either grab them with its needle-like teeth or grab them with its long tongue which was probably covered with sticky saliva. Desert dwelling insects like Dung Beetles have hard exoskeletons, and those sharp, pin-like teeth would be useful in grabbing the insect once it had been pulled to the mouth by the long, sticky-ended tongue.

E♯3
E♯4

E♯5
E♯6

E♯7
E♯8

Finally, this creature was not on the top of the food chain. It probably was hunted by larger animals. But to keep from getting eaten, it had big ears to pick up the sound of something sneaking up on it. Its eyes are out at the end of stalks and the creature uses them to look all around. That long nose can be stuck up into the air to pick up the scent of other creatures. Also, the creature had sharp spines on its back and on the end of its tail which are weapons for protection.

Thank you for considering my opinions. I would be happy to discuss this information with you further.

FIGURE 2.5. PERFORMANCE TASK ASSESSMENT LIST
CREATURE FEATURE

Element	Points Possible	Points Earned Assessment By: Self	Teacher	
1. A clear opinion has been stated as to the natural habitat of the creature.	10	10	10	*Excellent progress!*
2. At least five pieces of evidence are stated to substantiate the opinion.	20	20	20	
3. The relevance and importance of each piece of evidence is explained.	20	20	18	
4. An explanation is made as to how all the pieces of evidence "add up" to supporting the identification of the probably natural "home" of the creature.	10	10	5	*I only saw one place where you did this.*
5. Relevant personal experiences and previous learning is brought in to provide support.	10	10	10	
6. Labeled drawings are used to help present the evidence.	5	5	3 *no labels*	
7. Scientific words, when used, are explained.	5	5	4	
8. The writing, through its vocabulary, examples, and tone, is written as a paper from a scientist to other scientists.	5	4	3	
9. The mechanics of English are used correctly.	5	5	4	
10. The work is neat and presentable.	5	5	5	
11. The work is completed on time.	5	5	5	
Total	100	99	87	

B+

FIGURE 2.6. STUDENT'S SELF-REFLECTION

This is one of my best pieces of writing. I used a lot more details of information to explain my opinion. The examples of good writing on the plant test you showed us in class helped me to know how to use details and how to use what I already knew such as the similarities between the Creature and an elephant, and owl, and my dog. Another thing that was really helpful to me was my drawings. I did not think about how the water weeds would get in the way of the Creature's huge ears until I drew that little picture. I think that drawing helps me get more ideas to write about and I will try drawing more often.

FIGURE 2.7. TEACHER'S REFLECTIONS ON STUDENT RESPONSES TO THE CREATURE FEATURE TASK

For several years now a districtwide goal and a school-level objective has been to improve student performance in writing. Science focuses on expository writing because that is the form of writing best suited to this discipline. My personal objective for this year has been to improve student performance on short, content-rich essays that I use as part of many performance tasks and all major exams in Life Science class. I believe that writing is one of the most important ways students "construct" understanding and that writing is a window that I can use to analyze the depth of that understanding. Part of my action plan to accomplish my personal objective to improve students' expository writing included writing analyses of two writing tasks that I will use and the student performance resulting from them. These written analyses are part of my personal plan for professional development. I am on Phase II of the Teacher Evaluation Plan this year, and I have requested that my work to improve student performance and my written analyses be part of my evaluation.

My first round of analysis and reflection focuses on the *Creature Feature* task I used as a part of an exam for the unit "Structured for Survival" (the relationships among the structure and function of animals in the context of specific environments). I discuss the quality of this task, its assessment lists, and the instructional strategies I used to prepare my students for these types of written assignments. I summarize what I have learned about the students' understanding of the science concepts involved. Finally, from the analysis I made of the students' work, I describe my plans to continue to improve student performance in my Life Science class.

Note 1: For the purpose of this reflection, I chose the response of one student who began the year writing brief statements, which were generally on-target, but which were poorly supported with specific detail that would clarify his ideas. This student's writing is similar to the work of many students in my class.

The *Creature Feature* task was adapted from an item used on the 1996 Connecticut Academic Performance Test that was administered to all tenth-grade students. The district's science curriculum and assessment committee found the task to be well-connected to the content of our Life Science curriculum, which is itself well-connected to the Connecticut curriculum and performance standards in Science. (The *Creature Feature* task and its assessment list are a part of the collection of such tasks other Life Science teachers and I have at our disposal.) I used the task without having to change it, but made some adaptations to the assessment list. The original assessment list called for the student to use "sufficient" details to support their explanations. In my adapted list, I required the students to use at least five supporting details (item 2 on the assessment list) because I have been trying to get my students to use more details and explain their importance (item 3.) I find that when they push themselves to be more specific through the use and explanation of more details, their thinking shows more depth. Another change I made to the assessment list was to add an element that asked that students to use labeled drawings to support their explanations (item 6). I did this because the information teachers have received about multiple intelligences suggests that different students can construct knowledge and access it through different modalities. Now, my *Creature Feature* task assessment list calls for writing and drawing.

Prior to the unit exam of which the *Creature Feature* task was a part, I covered the three-week unit titled "Structured for Survival," which included readings from our text, three supplemental articles, and two laboratory activities. Some information was presented through lecture, at which time I modeled the use of drawings to augment my verbal and written explanations. I used cooperative learning strategies for the lab work, for homework checks, and for activities that I devised to show students how to use more details to support their written and drawn explanations of scientific concepts. The two-period unit exam contained multiple choice questions, several "label the parts" tasks, a question about the scientific method (related to one of the lab activities) and the *Creature Feature* task. I consider these unit exams to be as much a learning activity as they are tests.

The analysis of this student's response to the *Creature Feature* task shows me both the strengths of the instruction and how well the student understands scientific concepts, as well as the areas where improvements are needed. First, my emphasis on using more details really paid off. Most students used at least five accurate supporting details including details that made connections between the Creature and animals such as camels, elephants, owls, and dogs with which they were familiar. The student whose work I have attached used and explained eight details. Students have learned that the environment consists of biotic (plants, prey, and predators) and abiotic (temperature, water, and type of land surface) components. All students described details of the structure of the Creature and the physical characteristics of its habitat. All students made connections between the structure of the Creature and the types of food it eats. Most students made connections between the structure of the creature and the way it protected itself from predators.

Note 2: To get students to more accurately assess their own work, I required that students find and underline each supporting detail that they used. See the eight pieces of evidence labeled E1, E2, etc., in the student's work attached here. I was happy to see that the student accurately assessed his use and explanation of details.

Note 3. Many of the students described how helpful our study of the models of excellent writing to show how to use accurate details to support written explanations was. Also, three students in the class received help from the special education teacher in the Resource Room. These students commented on how they had learned to use a graphic organizer to help them put their ideas in order and to select the correct number of details to support each main idea. I think that I will get some advice from the special education teacher on how to make these graphic organizers so that all my students can benefit from this planning strategy.

Another high point was the student's use of drawings to support their written explanations. Several students, including this one, commented that making the drawings really helped them think more deeply about their explanations. The student whose work is attached discovered the relationship between the Creatures large ears and the problem of moving through the plants in a marsh or swamp by the picture that he drew.

Note 4: Most students picked a wet, marshy, or swampy environment as the natural habitat of the creature. The idea that the large ears are evidence against such an environment shows excellent analytical skills.

However, there are two areas of the students' responses that still frustrate me. One is the students' inability to explain how all "pieces of information"— the details—add up to be more powerful than any individual piece of data. The second is the students' inability to use the science vocabulary that they have been learning. Besides performing relatively poorly on those two aspects of the task, the student usually overestimated the quality of their work on these two parts of the assessment list. My discussion of these two areas of relative weaknesses will reveal my goals to make the adaptations necessary to bring these students to a higher level of understanding.

This student made one explicit statement at the end of paragraph three that tied two pieces of evidence together. Other connections were implied in paragraph four but not explicitly stated. From a review of the work done so far in class this year, I find that I have asked my students to use many accurate pieces of data to support their written explanations. However, I probably have not provided enough clear models of what I expect in regard to how pieces add up to tell a story that individual pieces cannot tell alone. Therefore, I will find or make examples of writing that both provide rich, supportive details and explain how the pieces work together to tell a story that none can do independently. Just as a study of the models of excellent use of details from the plant unit helped the students write better responses to details in the *Creature Feature* task, these new models should improve student performance on the writing tasks I will use during the unit on homeostasis, which comes up next.

The second area of concern is the inability of the students to use scientific vocabulary. Maybe this task did not lend itself to the use of the vocabulary. I will have to study that possibility. More likely, the students just did not pay attention to using the vocabulary. I may have to require that they make a list of the science vocabulary words that they plan to use and then underline the words that they do use in their written response.

Note 5: Several students in my class, including this one, decided to put their writing about the Creature in their writing folders to become candidates for inclusion in their writing portfolios, which are managed by the English teachers.

Finally, I would like to comment on the work that I have done to write this reflection and the help that I have received form other teachers. I spent approximately five hours over two days to write and revise this reflection. (I could not have done this without using a computer because I had to revise this reflection so much.) I would not want to do this too often, but I did find it a valuable experience as part of my personal professional-development plan. I found that having to express my thoughts through organized, detailed writing caused me to be much more conscious of the cause-effect relationships between my instructional materials and teaching strategies and my students' performance. Specifically, through this writing I "crystallized" the need to use more examples of excellent writing to show my students how to use many, accurate details and to explain how the details—when taken together—tell a more powerful story than when just presented as a collection of independent details.

Another insight I gained through this writing was that my original personal objective for the year was too broad. That objective was to "improve student performance on short, content-rich essays in science." This analysis of student work shows me that I need to focus on more focused components of writing, targeting one area at a time for improvement. I discovered that I did begin by focusing on the use of details to support ideas and that my work on that element did improve student performance. My next, more specific objective is to improve the way students explain how all the details add up to be more powerful than any of the details individually. I have learned to view writing as a set of components or skills. I can work on individual components during each assignment to improve student performance. Getting better at the individual components will give students the foundation for "putting it all together" so that their writing has "overall" quality.

This is the first reflection I have written and I did not know how to begin it. The opportunities to talk with other teachers about student work have been immensely valuable to me. I was beginning to feel overwhelmed because I thought that I needed to describe the work of all of my students. Looking at the reflections that have already been written in this school and in other schools in the district, showed me how to focus on one or two representative samples of student work and to organize a detailed description of what I did and how students performed. The assessment list for writing analyses and reflection helped me to remember what to include. The discussions with other teachers about these models of excellent reflections and the assessment list provided the guidance I needed. When I had tried to write reflections on student work before, I found myself going into detail about what I did and what students did, but I was not making explicit connections between the instruction and student learning. I feel good about this reflection because I learned to describe these cause-effect relationships (the impact of models on student performance) and to show specific examples of each (strong performance based on good models and poor performance due to the lack of models). I realize fully what it is like for student to be asked to use and explain details because I have had to be that explicit in this reflection.

Note 6: The after-school, interdepartmental sessions on how to analyze student work; the districtwide day for science teachers to work together; the time during the schoolwide in-service day that our science department had to work on learning strategies for performance-based learning and assessment; and the half-day of released time you provided to our study team to visit each other's classrooms was crucial to the progress I and my colleagues have made. Without this time, some work would have been accomplished, but we would not have made as much progress as we have. It was a very good idea for the teachers and the principal to plan in the fall how time would be provided during the school year for this work on curriculum, instruction, and assessment projects. Thank you for your support.

FIGURE 2.8. CREATURE MUSEUM

Background

You have successfully presented and defended your opinion regarding a natural habitat for the Creature. The museum staff has hired you to create a diorama that shows the Creature in that natural habitat.

Task

Your diorama is to be modeled after those that we saw at the Museum of Natural History. The diorama is to feature the Creature and include:

A. The Creature's favorite food species.

B. Flora including the species favored by the Creature's favorite food.

C. The main animal that preys on the Creature.

D. The most important characteristics of the physical environment in which the Creature lives.

The diorama may not be larger than 2.5 feet square and 18 inches high. Use the papier-mâché techniques we recently learned from the art teacher.

You are also required to write a script and make a five-minute audiotape that describes the ecology of your diorama.

Audience

The audience for your diorama and audiotape is the people who visit the museum.

Purpose

The purpose of your work is to present information on how animals interact with their environment and each other.

Procedure

1. Create the animal that is the main food source for the Creature.

2. Create the flora that is the main food source for the animals the creature eats.

3. Create the animal that preys on the Creature.

4.	Get your creations approved before you begin planning the diorama.

5.	Create a drawn plan for the diorama that shows how the plants and animals will be placed and what characteristics of the physical environment will be represented.

6.	Get your plan approved before you begin to construct your diorama.

7.	Construct your diorama.

8.	Write the script for your diorama's audiotape and have it approved before you record it.

9.	Record your script on audiotape. You may include sound effects.

Assessment

Refer to the assessment list that provides the criteria for each component of this project.

Scientific accuracy, attention to detail, clarity of explanation, creativity, craftsmanship, and good work habits are all assessed in this project.

FIGURE 2.9. PERFORMANCE TASK ASSESSMENT LIST
CREATURE MUSEUM

PREWRITING

Elements	Points Possible	Earned Assessment Self	Teacher
1. At least five life functions common to all mammals were listed.	____	____	____
2. External structures related to eating were listed in detail.	____	____	____
3. A guess was made about what kind of food the Creature ate based on its external structure.	____	____	____
4. External structures related to moving were listed in detail.	____	____	____
5. External structures related to sensing the environment were listed in detail.	____	____	____
6. External structures related to protection from the elements and from other organisms were listed in detail.	____	____	____
7. A guess was made about the details of the Creature's home environment (land, water, etc.) based on the Creature's external structures.	____	____	____
8. A guess was made about the kind of organisms that the Creature needed to be afraid of based on the Creature's external structure.	____	____	____
9. A guess was made about the Creature's place in the food web.	____	____	____
10. For each guess made, an explanation with details was given.	____	____	____
TOTAL:	____	____	____

Assessment Points appears above the Points Possible and Earned Assessment columns.

CREATURE'S FOOD

Elements	Points Possible	Earned Assessment Self	Teacher
1. Detailed structures that make this animal a consumer are shown and described.	____	____	____
2. Detailed structures that make this animal well suited to the environment are shown and described.	____	____	____
3. Overall, this animal appears to be a food source for the Creature.	____	____	____
4. The scale is appropriate.	____	____	____
5. Creativity is evident.	____	____	____
Subtotal—Creature's Food:	____	____	____

FLORA THAT IS THE FOOD SOURCE FOR THE CONSUMER

	Points Possible	Self	Teacher
6. Detailed structures that make this organism a plant are shown and described.	____	____	____
7. Detailed structures that make this plant well suited to this environment and to the consumer are shown and described.	____	____	____
8. The scale is appropriate.	____	____	____
9. Creativity is evident.	____	____	____
Subtotal—The Plant:	____	____	____

ANIMAL THAT PREYS ON THE CREATURE

	Points Possible	Self	Teacher
10. Detailed structures that make this animal a predator of the Creature are shown and described.	____	____	____
11. Detailed structures that make this predator well suited to this environment are shown and described.	____	____	____
12. The scale is appropriate.	____	____	____
13. Creativity is evident.	____	____	____
Subtotal—Predator of the Creature:	____	____	____

Assessment Points

DIORAMA OF THE CREATURE'S ENVIRONMENT

Elements	Assessment Points		
	Points Possible	Earned Assessment	
		Self	Teacher
14. Details of geography that are consistent with the description of the Creature's natural habitat are shown and described.	_____	_____	_____
15. Details of the elements of the physical environment are shown and described.	_____	_____	_____
16. The organisms that make up this food web are presented in the context of this environment and in a way that shows their relationship to each other.	_____	_____	_____
17. Color is used in a way that it would occur in this natural habitat.	_____	_____	_____
18. The diorama is sturdy and durable.	_____	_____	_____
19. The craftsmanship shows skill and attention to detail.	_____	_____	_____
20. Creativity is evident.	_____	_____	_____
Subtotal—The Diorama:	_____	_____	_____

THE SCRIPT FOR THE AUDIO TAPE

Elements	Points Possible	Self	Teacher
21. The script will provide a 5-minute audio tape.	_____	_____	_____
22. The script presents an interesting and friendly story.	_____	_____	_____
23. The physical environment is described in detail but without jargon.	_____	_____	_____
24. The concepts of the food web are presented clearly and accurately and without jargon.	_____	_____	_____
25. The concepts of the relationship of the structure of living things to their function are presented clearly and accurately and without jargon.	_____	_____	_____
26. Sufficient and accurate details are used.	_____	_____	_____
27. Analogies and references to what the "common person" would know help make the descriptions understandable.	_____	_____	_____
28. The script is well organized and there is an overall smooth flow to it.	_____	_____	_____
29. The mechanics of English are correct.	_____	_____	_____
30. The work is neat and presentable.	_____	_____	_____
Subtotal—The Script:	_____	_____	_____

THE AUDIO TAPE OF THE SCRIPT

Elements	Points Possible	Earned Assessment	
		Self	Teacher
31. The voice is clear and distinct.	_____	_____	_____
32. Proper grammar is used.	_____	_____	_____
33. Proper pronunciation is used.	_____	_____	_____
34. The rate of speech is appropriate.	_____	_____	_____
35. Inflections of the voice add interest.	_____	_____	_____
36. Creative sound effects are consistent with the science shown in this diorama.	_____	_____	_____
37. The audio tape lasts no more than 5 minutes.	_____	_____	_____
38. The sound quality of the audio tape is excellent.	_____	_____	_____
Subtotal—The Audio Tape:	_____	_____	_____

OVERALL WORK HABITS

39. All directions are followed.	_____	_____	_____
40. All checkpoints are reached on time.	_____	_____	_____
41. Feedback from self-assessment, peer assessment, and from the teacher is used to make improvements in the quality of the science presented and in the quality of the craftsmanship of the work.	_____	_____	_____
Subtotal—The Work Habits	_____	_____	_____
GRAND TOTAL:	_____	_____	_____

3

EMBEDDED PERFORMANCE TASKS USED BOTH FOR LEARNING AND ASSESSMENT

This chapter describes how performance tasks become part of instruction and not just an "add-on."

THE PROBLEM OF ASSESSMENT AS AN "ADD-ON"

We are all busy. Our teaching days are full. We do not need another "add-on," and that is what performance assessment sometimes seems to be. But performance tasks should be great learning activities put right where you want to use them in the curriculum. Performance tasks are often culminating activities helping students to learn how to use content knowledge, thinking skills, problem-solving skills, and work habits. Therefore, performance tasks are learning activities, not just assessment events. The *Creature Feature* task provides such an instructional activity and an opportunity for the student and the teacher to assess learning and teaching. Figures 3.1 and 3.2 present the "add-on" and the "embedded" models.

In Figure 3.1, the performance tasks, which are part of assessment, come after instruction is over. In this model, the performance tasks are "add-ons" and compete for time with instruction. In Figure 3.2, the performance task is embedded in instruction and becomes part of the mix of strategies and activities in the context of teaching and learning for that unit.

All of the performance tasks in this book are intended to be both embedded learning activities and opportunities to assess student work at the same time.

FIGURE 3.1. PERFORMANCE TASKS AS ADD-ONS

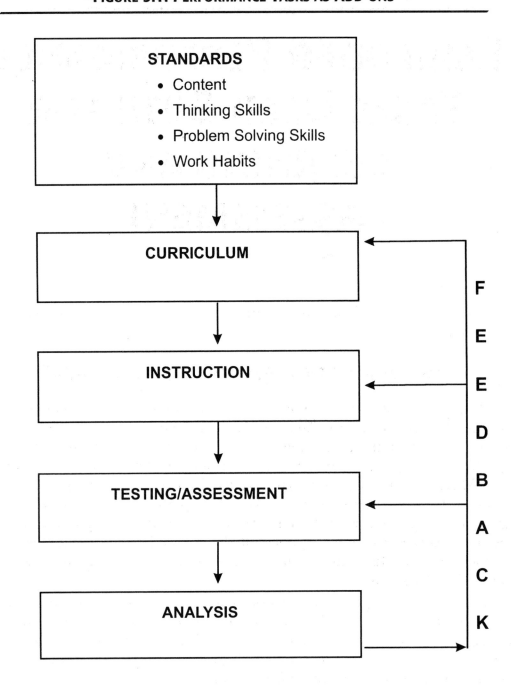

FIGURE 3.2. PERFORMANCE TASKS EMBEDDED IN INSTRUCTION

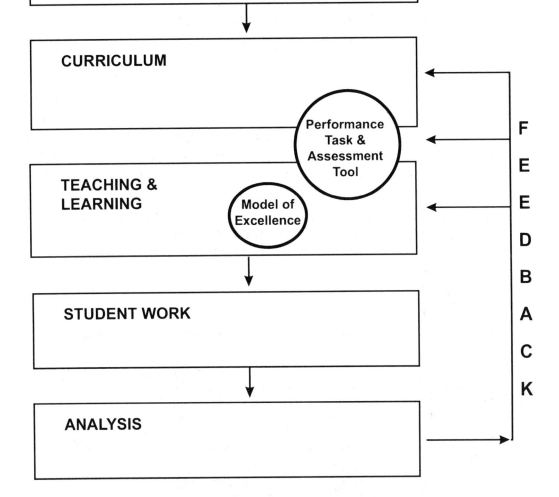

THE PROBLEM OF THE MATCH BETWEEN CURRICULUM AND INSTRUCTION: IS THE WRITTEN CURRICULUM THE TAUGHT CURRICULUM?

One of the problems that educators face is that the curriculum documents are "set aside" and classroom instruction goes its own direction. The "taught curriculum," in that case, does not match the "written curriculum." Figure 3.2 shows that a performance task such as *Creature Feature* and its assessment list are embedded in instruction. The *Creature Feature* task has been written to be well connected to content, thinking skill, problem-solving, and work habit standards for the curriculum (Grade 7 Life Science) which it serves. Therefore, when the *Creature Feature* task is used as a task for learning and assessment, teaching is better connected to the curriculum, which is, in turn, based on standards.

HOW EMBEDDED PERFORMANCE TASKS INFLUENCE TEACHING

Figure 3.3 shows that the performance task and its assessment list are a culminating activity and the arrow indicates that the teacher plans backward through the unit to create lessons that prepare the student for the performance task. Using backward planning also balances teacher-directed instruction, group work, individual study, hands-on labs, work on the computer and in the media center, tests and quizzes, and performance tasks within the entire unit of instruction.

FIGURE 3.3. A UNIT OF INSTRUCTION IN A SCIENCE COURSE

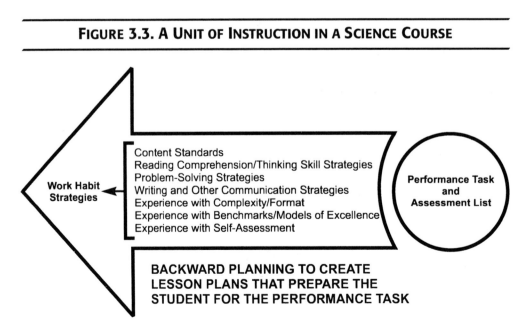

If you were the teacher using the Grade 7 Life Science Curriculum, you would make a decision as to which performance task or tasks to use in each unit. (Unit 4: Structured for Survival has three performance tasks and *Creature Feature* is one of them.) You would select the performance task you planned to use at the end of the unit before you began that unit. Therefore, knowing that *Creature Feature* would be the culminating activity would help you plan what you would do during the entire unit.

The instruction that precedes the *Creature Feature* would include work on the science content of how external body plans support life functions within specific environments. Instruction would also focus on the thinking skill of making and supporting inferences and on the writing process including using concept map graphic organizers. Finally, the work habit of paying attention to details gets some attention. Thus, the performance task strongly influences the instruction that comes before it.

SUMMARY

Chapter 3 describes performance tasks as both embedded learning activities and as opportunities to assess student performance.

4

CURRICULUM STANDARDS FOR PERFORMANCE TASKS

Question 1 in Chapter 1 asked, "What should students know and be able to do?" This question leads us to the development of curriculum standards that identify the important content and process skills that will serve as the foundation for a curriculum. The *Creature Feature* task requires the student to know the relevant science content, to make detailed observations, to make and support an inference, to use the writing process, and to manage time well. *Creature Feature* was valid because it was well connected to standards. A deficiency in any of these standards will cause the student to "miss the mark."

This chapter demonstrates some of the curriculum standards that are important to a seventh grade biology class in which the *Creature Feature* performance task is used.

CONTENT STANDARDS FOR SCIENCE

Sets of national standards for science include:

♦ Project 2061's *Benchmarks for Science Literacy* published by the American Association for the Advancement of Science (AAAS)

♦ *Scope, Sequence, and Coordination of Secondary School Science: The Content Core* published by the National Science Teachers Association (NSTA)

♦ *The National Science Education Standards* published by the National Research Council (NRC)

♦ *The Science Framework* published by the National Assessment of Educational Progress (NAEP)

♦ The New Standards Project's published standards in science and other disciplines

John S. Kendall and Robert J. Marzano published *Content Standards: A Compendium of Standards and Benchmarks for K-12 Education, 2nd Edition*, as a collaborative project of the Mid-continent Regional Educational Laboratory (McREL) and the Association for Supervision and Curriculum Development (ASCD). Curriculum standards for the performance tasks in this book are taken from that McREL compendium. Figure 4.1 shows the content standard and benchmark relevant to *Creature Feature.*

FIGURE 4.1. CURRICULUM STANDARDS FOR THE CREATURE FEATURE TASK

SCIENCE STANDARD 4, K–12

- Knows about the unity and diversity that characterizes life

- Benchmark for Level III (Grades 6–8)

  Knows that animals and plants have a great variety of body plans and internal structures that serve specific functions for survival (e.g., digestive structures in vertebrates, invertebrates, unicellular organisms, and plants)

LANGUAGE ARTS WRITING STANDARD 1, K–12

- Demonstrates competence in the general skills and strategies of the writing process

- Benchmarks for Level III (Grades 6–8)

  1. *Prewriting:* Uses a variety of prewriting strategies (e.g., makes outlines, uses published pieces as writing models, constructs critical standards, brainstorms, builds background knowledge)

  2. *Drafting and Revising:* Uses a variety of strategies to draft and revise written work (e.g., analyzes and clarifies meaning, makes structural and syntactical changes; uses an organizational scheme; uses sensory words and figurative language; rethinks and rewrites for different audiences and purposes; checks for a consistent point of view and for transitions between paragraphs; uses direct feedback to revise compositions)

  3. Writes expository compositions (e.g., presents information that reflects knowledge about the topic of the report; organizes and presents information in a logical manner.

Reproduced by permission from John S. Kendall and Robert J. Marzano, *Content Knowledge: A Compendium of Standards and Benchmarks K-12, 2nd ed.,* pp. (also known as the "McREL Standards").

LANGUAGE ARTS STANDARDS FOR SCIENCE

Writing is a foundation literacy skill for performance-based learning and assessment in all disciplines. Many performance tasks used in the classroom ask students to produce a written product or written plans for a product such as an invention or a performance such as an oral presentation. Written responses are required on some state and national tests. Therefore, writing is emphasized in this book and standards relevant to writing are identified for performance tasks. Figure 4.1 shows the writing standard and benchmarks relevant to *Creature Feature*.

Creature Feature requires expository writing, that is, writing to inform, explain, or teach. The collection of tasks in Appendix A shows many more tasks that require some form of expository writing and a few tasks that ask for persuasive writing. Appendix C contains frameworks and scoring tools for many kinds of student work, including persuasive and narrative writing.

THINKING SKILLS FOR SCIENCE

In addition to the content standards and language arts standards from the McREL compendium, the performance tasks in this book are connected to thinking skills such as sequencing, inferring, predicting, comparing, and judging.

This book also uses a framework of thinking-skill verbs, which are organized into four categories. The entire framework of verbs is presented in Chapter 5.

One example of a verb from each of the four thinking-skill categories is shown here. The verb is part of the statement of a performance task.

Category 1:   Initial Understanding
                SEQUENCE the events in photosynthesis.

Category 2:   Developing an Interpretation
                PREDICT what would happen to the food web if a
                virus attacked and destroyed chloroplasts.

Category 3:   Making Connections
                RELATE what you just learned about the process of
                rusting to the process of respiration that we studied
                earlier this year.

Category 4:   Taking a Critical Stance
                JUDGE the validity and reliability of the results of
                an experiment relating the color of light to the rigors
                of plant growth.

PROBLEM-SOLVING PROCESS
PERFORMANCE STANDARDS

Any science performance task that involves writing uses a form of problem solving called the "Writing Process." Other forms of problem solving important to the science classroom are the scientific method, inventing, modeling, and math problem solving. Frameworks for writing and these other versions of problem-solving techniques are found in Appendix C. Performance tasks using the scientific method are found in Chapter 7 and performance tasks using other forms of problem-solving are in Appendix A.

WORK HABIT AND PERFORMANCE TASKS

When students are engaged in a performance task, work habits are a part of their overall performance. All work requires work habits and the poor performance of some students is due more to deficiencies in work habits than to what they know. Work habits include:

♦ Following directions

♦ Paying attention to the details

♦ Managing time

♦ Being organized

♦ Working with others

♦ Persisting

♦ Assessing one's own work accurately

♦ Setting and carrying out goals to improve

Sometimes a work habit is assessed directly (directions were followed and the work was turned in on time), and sometimes the work habit is assessed through its influence on another aspect of the work (a data chart format is created that is simple, clear, and organized.)

PERFORMANCE TASKS INTEGRATE KNOWLEDGE
OF SCIENCE CONTENT, THINKING SKILLS,
PROBLEM-SOLVING SKILLS, AND WORK HABITS

Real work requires that a worker have specific content knowledge, use thinking skills such as sequencing or predicting, employ problem-solving strategies such as the writing process or the scientific method, and have productive work habits. One characteristic of performance tasks is that they mirror work done in the "real world," which makes performance tasks in the science classroom well-connected to the knowledge of the content of science and to general processes such as thinking skills, writing, and work habits.

THEMES, BIG IDEAS, AND ESSENTIAL QUESTIONS OF SCIENCE ALSO SERVE AS PERFORMANCE STANDARDS

Another approach to the content of science is through the themes, big ideas, and essential questions of science. Figure 4.2 shows the five themes used by the Region 15 Public Schools in Connecticut to organize their K–12 science curriculum.

FIGURE 4.2. REGION 15 SCIENCE THEMES GRADES 1–12

Science (S)

All phenomena will be viewed through a systems framework.

A system can be studied through one or more of these themes:

I. Learning about a system through studying its attributes of size, scale, diversity, distribution and normality.

II. Learning about a system through studying the relationship between its function and structure.

III. Learning about a system through studying the patterns of changes of its matter and energy.

IV. Learning about systems through experimenting, modeling and inventing.

V. Learning about the special systems of society, science and technology.

This approach uses these five themes as ways of organizing information in all science courses from Kindergarten through grade 12. Each theme is a way of looking at any component of the science curriculum, including topics in biology, chemistry, physics, earth science, and space science. All five themes approach science as a study of "systems." A system is anything you define it as. The population in your school is a system, as is one student, one body system, one tissue within that body system, one cell, one organelle, one molecule, one atom, and so on. Each system can be studied through the "lens" of one or more of these five themes.

The *Creature Feature* task is designed to be connected to theme II, "Learning About a System (the Creature) Through Studying the Relationship Between Its Function and Structure." In this performance task, the student is asked to describe how the external body plan (the structure) helps the Creature carry out its life functions (the function) within the context of a specific environment.

The hope is that after many years of viewing phenomena in all fields of science through this "structure/function" perspective, students will see any system that way on their own.

SAMPLE OF A SEVENTH GRADE BIOLOGY CURRICULUM THAT IS ORGANIZED AROUND PERFORMANCE STANDARDS

These five science themes are abstracts and stated in that form. They must be restated more concretely and specifically within the context of specific units of study to be made meaningful. Figure 4.3 lists eight Essential Questions that are the focus for a whole year of study in a Grade 7 Life Science course. The roman numerals in parentheses after each question indicate to which of the five science themes that essential question relates. Notice that Essential Questions 2, 3, and 4 are related to theme II regarding structure and function.

FIGURE 4.3. BIOLOGY GRADE 7 IN REGION 15 SCHOOLS
ESSENTIAL QUESTIONS FOR THE YEAR

---

1. How can graphs help us understand the attributes of size, scale, diversity, distribution, and normality of living things? (I)

2. What life functions must all living things, from cells to whole organisms, carry out? (Function aspect of II)

3. What are the most amazing examples of how the structures of living things, from cells to whole organisms, enable those living things to carry out their life functions? (II)

4. How does the environment influence the structures of living things, from cells to whole organisms? (II)

5. How true are these two statements? (III)
   Matter continues to be recycled in nature.
   Energy moves through nature but is not recycled.

6. How have the inventions of humans changed the environment? Are these changes good or bad? (V)

7. How can we use models to learn more about the concept of "form follows function"? (IV)

8. Why do scientists believe that what they call "a scientific method" is a good way to solve problems? (IV)

Although the Essential Questions are more specific than the Themes, they are still not specific enough for day-to-day instruction. Figure 4.4 shows the first page of Unit 4 in that Grade 7 Life Science course. There are three focus questions for this unit, which is called "Structured for Survival." These are the three questions that direct the student's thinking within Unit 4. The numerals in parentheses after each focus question show the Essential Question to which each Focus Question is connected. Focus Question B is connected to Essential Question 2, which is, in turn, connected to Theme II, regarding structure and function.

FIGURE 4.4. FIRST PAGE UNIT 4 IN A GRADE 7 LIFE SCIENCE COURSE

UNIT 4: STRUCTURED FOR SURVIVAL

FOCUS QUESTIONS FOR THE UNIT

A. What are the ranges of each factor in the environment that are important to the survival of living organisms? (1)

B. How have organisms evolved structures to carry out their life functions in different environments? (2, 3, 4)

C. How can models help us understand the relationships among structures and functions? (7)

CONTENT PERFORMANCE STANDARDS (*from the Connecticut Science Curriculum Standards*)

Content Standard 5: Relationships of Structure and Function

Performance Standards:

5.6 Identify anatomical and behavioral adaptations that allow organisms to survive in specific environments.

5.7 Explain how the features of living things can be good indicators of their role and place in an ecosystem.

5.11 Describe ways in which internal and external body structures and body plans contribute to an organism's ability to carry out life functions and processes.

5.14 Understand the complementary nature of structure and function.

5.15 Describe how different life functions are carried out by different organisms.

PERFORMANCE TASKS

a. A Gallery of Graphs (A)

b. Creature Features (B)

c. Marvelous Models (C)

Unit 4, "Structured for Survival," has three performance tasks from which the science teacher may choose:

♦ *A Gallery of Graphs*

♦ *Creature Features*

♦ *Marvelous Models*

The *Creature Feature* task is connected to Focus Question B of this unit, "How have organisms evolved structures to carry out their life functions in different environments?"

Thus, *Creature Feature* task is well connected to both content standards and to themes, and is a way to determine whether students can use the science information they have been learning.

WHY THEMES AND CONTENT STANDARDS?

Content standards tend to be about specific topics within the discipline of science. Attention to standards helps us focus our attention on what is important to learn about such topics as cells, whole organisms, atomic particles, the earth, and the solar system. Themes help us pay attention to the connections among these topics. Structure/function is one way to see connections among these topics. The more connections that students see, the deeper their understanding of these topics. We are trying to support deep understanding of science, not just surface-level knowledge. We need to pay attention to the pieces, the content standards, and the whole—the themes.

5

How to Make a Performance Task

Question 2 in Chapter 1 asked, "What kinds of tests shall we construct to see how well students perform?" Tests include the entire range of instruments from information-level multiple choice tests to long-term research projects. This book focuses on the construction and use of open-ended performance tasks that take two to five class periods to complete.

This chapter explains how to make a performance task and discusses these three topics:

- ♦ Definitions and Dimensions of Performance Tasks

- ♦ Strategies for Coming Up with Ideas for Performance Tasks

- ♦ Strategies for Making Classroom-Friendly Performance Tasks from Those Ideas

Definitions and Dimensions for Performance Tasks

Some of the terms that are used in this chapter are defined below.

Term	*Definition*
Performance Task	A task that requires students to use content knowledge, thinking skills, problem-solving skills, and work habits to produce a product and/or a performance. In this book, a performance task is considered a culminating learning activity and a type of open-ended test.
Authentic Performance	A performance task that puts students into real or task-simulated situations to create products and/or performances for actual or simulated audiences. Although the teacher and peers can be audiences, authentic performance tasks attempt to use other audiences.

Term	Definition
Embedded Performance Task	A performance task that is placed in day-to-day instruction just when and where it should be used to be a great learning activity and an opportunity to assess the student's performance.
Equitable Performance	A performance task that is equitable is "fair" because task students have had the opportunity to learn the content knowledge, the thinking skills, the problem-solving skills, and the work habits on which the performance task is based. A performance task is "fair" because the level of complexity of the task is reasonable for the experience the student has had with performance tasks. A performance task is "fair" because the examples and specific information used in the task are within the experience of that student.
Manageable Performance Task	A performance task that is worth the instructional time and effort it takes and is user-friendly for the teacher.
Valid Performance Task	A performance task that is actually connected to the content standards, thinking skills, problem-solving skills, and work habits for which it is intended.

DIMENSIONS OF A GOOD PERFORMANCE TASK

How do you know if a performance task you find or make is a good one? Figure 5.1 presents 13 dimensions of a performance task. You can use this list of dimensions to make an assessment tool to help you judge the quality of performance tasks.

FIGURE 5.1. THIRTEEN DIMENSIONS OF A PERFORMANCE TASK

Dimension	Explanation
Activating	The more the student works on the task, the more the student is drawn into the task.
Authentic Process	The steps in the performance task mirror those steps taken by a person in the "larger world" creating a similar product or performance for a similar audience.
Authentic Product	The product and/or performance, which the student is making or giving, are similar to products and/or performances made or given in the "larger world."
Embedded	Used within instruction rather than an "add-on" to it.

Dimension	Explanation
Engaging	Grabs the student's attention.
Equitable	Is "fair" to students based on their background knowledge and their experience with performance tasks.
Essential	Connected to the most important content standards rather than trivial ones.
Feasible	Possible to do given the constraints of time and resources and is safe.
Feedback & Revision Loop	The performance task lets the student make revisions. This may occur through an informal process of self-assessment and revision during a first draft, or it may occur as a process whereby the student gets feedback from peers and/or the teacher on a first draft and then completes a second draft.
Group Work & Individual Work	Uses the right balance of group work and individual work. Most performance tasks require individual work. Group work, if it is used at all during the actual performance task, is used in an early step in the task.
Appropriate Structure	The task, including its graphic organizers and the assessment tool, has the right amount explanation built into it based on the experience the student has had with performance task.
Integrative	Ties elements of real work together: Content Knowledge, Thinking Skills, Problem-Solving Skills, such as the writing process, and Work Habits.
Promotes Deeper Understanding	Expects students to go beyond surface-level knowledge to show the depth of their understanding of science.

COMING UP WITH IDEAS FOR PERFORMANCE TASKS

Before we can create a performance task to use we must get ideas for tasks. The tasks must meet the criteria for excellent tasks. Most performance tasks are shaped and sharpened from projects that you already do. Sometimes all that is needed is to add an assessment list to the task. The assessment lists in this book provide ideas and models for assessment lists that will work with your tasks and your students. Following are four strategies for getting ideas for performance tasks.

The ideas for performance tasks presented in this section are just the first step in building a performance task. Each idea must be shaped, focused, and structured into a classroom-friendly performance task. The next section shows how to take an idea and turn it into such a performance task.

STRATEGY #1: QUESTIONS THAT ACT AS GUIDES TO CREATION OF PERFORMANCE TASKS

The following questions are guides to help you come up with ideas for performance tasks. Each question is followed by an idea for a performance task that is relevant to that question.

- ◆ **Does the task ask students to use accurate information from the current unit to explain and/or interpret?**

  - Explain how smoking influences the structure and function of the lung.

- ◆ **Does the task ask students to use accurate information from several units to explain and/or interpret?**

  - This year we have studied the structure and function of lungs, gills, and spherical respiratory systems of insects. What are the common principles of structure and function that are true of all three of these systems?

- ◆ **Does the task ask the students to confront misconceptions?**

  - When asked why it is hot in the summer and cold in the winter in New England, many people explain that the sun is closer to the earth in the summer and further from the earth in the winter. Is this explanation correct? Explain why or why not this explanation of the seasons is scientifically correct. Use diagrams and written explanations.

- ◆ **Does the task ask the students to approach the topic from a unique or unusual point of view?**

  - We have learned about how scientists are "genetically engineering" potatoes so that the potato plants will manufacture their own insecticide. We have learned why the some potato farmers like this new type of potato. But some potato farmers think that this "genetically engineered" potato is a bad idea. Explain the arguments of both points of view.

- ◆ **Does the task ask the student to apply the information to some aspect of his or her own life?**

  - How good is your diet? Take the role of a nutritionist and analyze your diet. Write a report to yourself explaining the "good news" and the "bad news" of your diet. Finish the report with recommendations for improving your diet.

- ◆ **Does the task ask the student to construct a theory or generalization true to the information?**

  - We have been studying the behavior of mammals and have just seen a movie about the behavior of wolves. (The sound was turned off so that the students did not hear the narration for the movie.) Make at least three generalizations about the behavior of wolves and support your generalizations with specific references to the behaviors you saw in the movie. You may also use information from our study of chimpanzees.

- ◆ **Does the task ask the student to ask insightful questions about the topic?**

  - We have concluded a chapter about global warming and are expecting a visit from a scientist to tell us more about this topic. What questions would you like answered about global warming? Brainstorm your questions and then organize them into categories. Each category must have a title. Finally, if you could ask only one question about global warming what would it be and why is that question so important?

- ◆ **Does the task ask the student to judge the quality of another person's use of science information or theories?**

  - We have seen the movie *Aliens*. According to what we know about life cycles, food webs, and how external body plans support the function of the organism in particular environments, some of the concepts presented in *Aliens* are plausible and some are not. Overall, did the creators of *Aliens* do a good job or a bad job of using correct science in that movie? Assume the role of a scientist movie critic and explain the "good science" and the "bad science" in *Aliens*.

STRATEGY #2: THINKING-SKILL VERBS PROVIDE STRATEGIES TO CREATE PERFORMANCE TASKS

Another way to create or shape and sharpen tasks is to use the thinking-skill verb list in Figure 5.2, which presents a four-part framework of thinking-skill verbs. Organizations such as the National Association of Education Progress (NAPE) and state departments of education use these four categories, or categories much like them, to define reading comprehension. Each of the four levels is a way of looking at how students understand what they have read (or seen and heard.)

An idea for a performance task is listed for each of the four levels of reading comprehension to show how the verbs can "assess" understanding from the point of view of each category. A simple performance task uses one of these verbs while a more complex and longer task uses verbs from more than one category in the framework.

- ♦ **Initial Understanding Verbs**

    The verbs in this part of the framework are for performance tasks that are intended to determine the degree to which students literally understand what they are learning.

    - Identify and sequence through labeled drawings the food web we studied that involved dairy cattle.

- ♦ **Developing an Interpretation Verbs**

    The verbs in this part of the framework are for performance tasks that are intended to determine how well students can extend and apply what they learned through such actions as making inferences and predictions, analyzing cause and effect, constructing generalizations, creating analogies, or comparing and contrasting.

    - Infer the natural habitat of this Creature.

        The *Creature Feature* task asks the students to make and support an inference as to the natural habitat of the Creature based on the Creature's external body plan.

- ♦ **Making Connections Verbs**

    The Developing an Interpretation area of the framework is about processing information within the context of the current unit of study. Making Connections is about relating *information in the current unit of study* to information in a *previous unit of study* ("Compare the structure of a plant's circulatory system to that of an animal.") in

---

FIGURE 5.2. READING COMPREHENSION ACTION VERBS
DEFINE THINKING SKILLS

INITIAL UNDERSTANDING (Literal Understanding)

Calculate	Display	Label	Make	Sequence
Compute	Examine	List	Match	Show
Describe	Identify	Locate	Recall	Summarize
Demonstrate				

DEVELOPING AN INTERPRETATION

Add to	Contrast	Examine	Make Analogies
Analyze	Decide	Explain	Paraphrase
Apply	Defend	Extend	Predict
Categorize	Describe Patterns	Extrapolate	Prioritize
Challenge	Describe Relationships	Generalize	Respond
Classify	Design	Guess	Revise
Combine	Devise	Hypothesize	Support
Compare	Discuss	Infer	Synthesize
Complete	Dissect	Integrate	Use Metaphors
Conclude	Documenting	Interpret	Use Similes
Confirm	Draw Conclusions	Justify	Uncover
Construct			

MAKING CONNECTIONS (between what you already know and the new information)

Add to	Contrast	Examine	Make Analogies
Analyze	Decide	Explain	Paraphrase
Apply	Defend	Extend	Predict
Categorize	Describe Patterns	Extrapolate	Prioritize
Challenge	Describe Relationships	Generalize	Respond
Classify	Design	Guess	Revise
Combine	Devise	Hypothesize	Support
Compare	Discuss	Infer	Synthesize
Complete	Dissect	Integrate	Use Metaphors
Conclude	Documenting	Interpret	Use Similes
Confirm	Draw Conclusions	Justify	Uncover
Construct			

CRITICAL STANCE

Check	Dissect	Integrate	Rate
Criticize	Evaluate	Judge	Support
Dispute	Identify Error	Rank	

another course ("In biology, we learned that lungs and kidneys operate on the structure/function principle of increasing surface area to increase efficiency of exchange. Where do we find the same structure/function principle operating in chemistry? Where do we find that same structure/function principle operating in how humans create cities and towns?"), *or to the student's "real life" experience* ("Analyze your various positions in the food web after a class picnic where various insects, such as mosquitos, were a problem.").

♦ **Taking a Critical Stance Verbs**

The verbs in this part of the framework are for performance tasks intended to see how well the student can judge or critique the explanations or theories of another person.

• Eric Carle wrote *The Very Hungry Caterpillar*, a famous children's book. Overall, did Eric Carle do a good job or bad job of using science in this book? Take the role of a scientist book critic, and identify and explain the "good science" and the "bad science" in this book.

STRATEGY #3: IDEAS FOR FORMATS OF FINAL PRODUCTS AND/OR PERFORMANCES

Figures 5.3 through 5.6 (pp. 49 and 50) provide ideas for performance tasks. Review each figure and glean ideas from them.

Another strategy that helps stimulate ideas for performance tasks is to review a list of various types of products and performances that might be built into a performance task. An added benefit of using Figure 5.3 for ideas for performance tasks is that the performance tasks become more authentic. The final product in the *Creature Feature* task was to write a letter to "other scientists." The final product might have been more authentic, that is, more like a real task to students, if that task had required the student to play the role of scientist and write an article for a children's science magazine about the Creature.

Performance tasks often ask students to communicate what they know through their writing, drawing, speaking, or constructions to an audience other than the teacher and classmates. When the student is actually writing a chapter for a book to be given to third graders, the task becomes authentic and more engaging without losing any of its content rigor.

The list of intended impacts shows that the performance task may ask the student to explain, teach, persuade, or judge. Products and performances in the real world are always intended to impact some audience in a particular way. Performance tasks help students learn to present what they know in different

---

FIGURE 5.3. FORMATS FOR PRODUCTS AND PERFORMANCES

Many of the entries in these lists can be final products, parts of final products, or intermediate products that support a final product or performance.

Graphic Organizers
Cause and Effect Sequence or Web
Character Analysis Frameworks
Classification Keys
Concept Maps
Cycles
Decision-Making Flow Charts
Flow Charts
Outlines
Pro/Con or Strengths/Weaknesses Charts
Story Boards
Story Webs
Time Lines

Performances
Conflict Resolution, Mediation
Dance
Debate
Group Work, Collaboration
Interview
Music, Vocal, and/or Instrumental
Newscast
Panel Discussion
Puppet Show
Skit
Speech, Oral Presentation
Video

Other Organizational Products
Assessment Lists
Blueprints
Designs
Double Entry Journals
Goals and Objectives
Data Charts
Diaries
Note Cards
Observation Logs
Plans
Tables
Time and Task Management Plans

Graphs
Bar Graph
Box and Whisker Graph
Histogram
Line Graph
Pictograph
Pie or Circle Graph
Scatter Gram
Stem and Leaf Plot

Written Products With and Without Graphics
Analogy
Biography
Brochure
Business Letter
Consumer Newsletter
Explanation, Directions
Friendly Letter
Memos
Nature Myth
Painting
Persuasive Letter
Portfolio
Questions
Resumes
Sequels
Test
Autobiography
Book
Bulletin Board
Cartoons
Drawing with Explanation
Fable
Home Page
Menus
Newspaper
Pamphlet
Photograph(s) with Explanation
Poster
Recipes
Self-Reflection Analysis
Short Story
Banner
Book Report
Bumper Sticker
Chapter of a Book
Essay
Fairy Tale
Letter to the Editor
Metaphor
Obituary
Paragraph
Poem
Proposal
Report
Sentence
Song Lyrics

Constructed Products
Apparatus
Collages
Costume
Display
Food
Invention
Machine
Model
Museum Display, Diorama
Puppet
Sculpture
Tool

FIGURE 5.4. OPTIONS FOR AUDIENCE FOR THE FINAL PRODUCT OR PERFORMANCE

Adult in the School, not the Teacher
Artist
Author
Boss
Business Person
Character in a Book, Poem, Movie, or Video
Classroom Teacher
Consumer of a Product or a Service
Editor
Employee
Engineer
Government Official
Grandparent or Other Relative: Past, Present, Future

Historical Character: Past, Present, Future
Illustrator
Judge
Juvenile Member of the Family
Member of an Advocacy Group
Museum or Gallery Visitor
Parent
Political Candidate
Principal or other Administrator
Private Foundation
Scientist
Students in Your Class
Students in Your School
Students in Another School
Younger Children

FIGURE 5.5. OPTIONS FOR PURPOSE—INTENDED IMPACT OF THE PRODUCT OR PERFORMANCE ON THE AUDIENCE

Arouse to Action	Explain	Inspire	Teach
Entertain	Inform	Persuade	

FIGURE 5.6. SOME OPTIONS FOR THE ROLE OF THE STUDENT MAKING THE PRODUCT OR GIVING THE PERFORMANCE

Advertiser
Animal
Artist
Athlete
Atom
Author
Autobiographer
Biographer
Body System
Business Person
Candidate
Cell
Citizen

Consumer
Detective
Director of a Museum or Art Gallery
The Earth
Engineer
Eyewitness
Famous Person: Past, Present, Future
Fictitious Person: Past, Present, Future
Government Official: Past, Present, Future
Inventor
Judge
Lawyer
Literary Critic

Machine
Molecule
Newscaster
Plant
Police Officer
Reporter
Trades Person
Travel Agent
Tutor
Tour Guide
Zoo Keeper

ways to different audiences. One outcome of performance-based learning and assessment is this increased sense of audience.

Finally, the list of roles students may simulate or actually play provides even more ideas for shaping performance tasks.

STRATEGY #4: THE THEORY OF MULTIPLE INTELLIGENCES GIVES US IDEAS FOR PERFORMANCE TASKS

Using a variety of formats for student products and performances over the year also addresses the topic of Multiple Intelligences. Figure 5.3 (p. 49) includes products and performances that connect to the framework for Multiple Intelligences presented by Howard Gardner. Following is a list of some intelligences and a product or performance that corresponds to it.

Type of Intelligence	*Format for Product or Performance*
Linguistic	Write a children's story about the growth of a plant and use the format for a short story: Beginning, Rising Action, High Point, Ending. Use accurate science.
Logical-Mathematical	Create a flowchart that shows how a hamburger is digested. You may use the computer to create and display this flowchart.
Spatial	Create a three-dimensional model of the structure of a river basin. Define the function of each part.
Body-Kinesthetic	Perform a skit that shows how heat energy influences molecules.
Musical	Write and perform a piece of music that demonstrates the principle that for every action there is an equal and opposite reaction.
Interpersonal	Select a scientist who proposed a theory that was very controversial. In a group of three, take the role of the scientist, the prosecuting attorney, or the defense attorney. Put that scientist on trial for promoting that controversial theory.
Intrapersonal	Keep a personal log of how your body temperature, heart beat, and "level of energy" varies throughout a 48-hour period. Relate this biorhythm data to your lifestyle.

MAKING CLASSROOM-FRIENDLY PERFORMANCE TASKS FROM THOSE IDEAS

Once we have ideas for performance tasks, they must be engineered into the actual performance tasks for students. Figure 5.7 (p. 53) presents a framework for making a performance task. Although there is not just one sequence of steps to using this framework, the sequence described here is commonly used. Figure 5.7 can be thought of as a graphic organizer for the initial planning stage of a performance task. Once notes have been made on the framework (Fig. 5.8, p. 54), Figure 5.9 (p. 55) is used to record the specifics of the performance task. (Figure 5.9 is a formal way to record the specifics of the performance task when tasks are being made and shared by many teachers in a school district. Classroom teachers who are making performance tasks for their own use may not need this step.)

These are the components of the framework in Figure 5.7:

- ◆ Content

  The first step is to state the essential or focus question and the content standards on which the performance task is to be based. A performance task is valid if it really gets at the understanding based on that question and those standards. Throughout the process of creating and revising the performance task and its assessment list, the author must continually ask, "Is this task clearly related to the content?" Colleagues help by giving their opinion as to the validity of our performance tasks. The content standards for the *Creature Feature* performance task were presented in Figure 4.1 (p. 34).

- ◆ Final Product or Performance (Fig. 5.3, p. 49)

  Usually, the next step is to visualize what the final product and/or performance of the task is to be. Deciding on a newspaper article, persuasive letter, annotated diagram on a poster, three-dimensional model with a written explanation, or an oral presentation with visuals gives the performance task a concrete shape that can then be worked into a manageable and equitable performance task.

- ◆ Audience, Purpose, and Role of the Learner (Figs. 5.4, 5.5, and 5.6, p. 50)

  Along with selecting the format for the final product and/or performance, the audience, purpose, and role of the learner are identified. These decisions about format, audience, purpose, and role are what make the task engaging to students.

(Text continues on page 56.)

**FIGURE 5.7. ELEMENTS OF A PERFORMANCE-BASED
LEARNING/ASSESSMENT TASK**

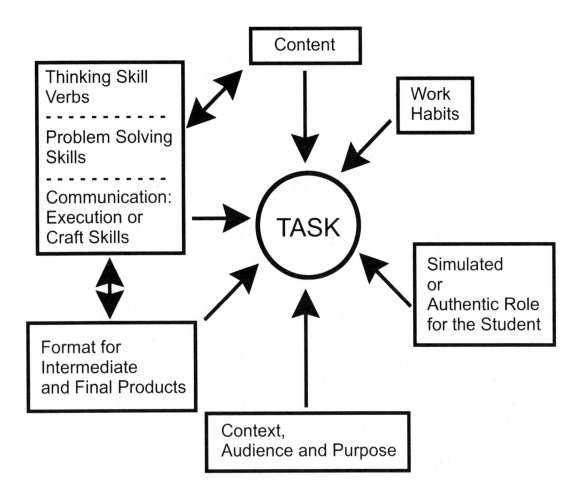

FIGURE 5.8. PLANNING THE *CREATURE FEATURE* TASK USING THE FRAMEWORK

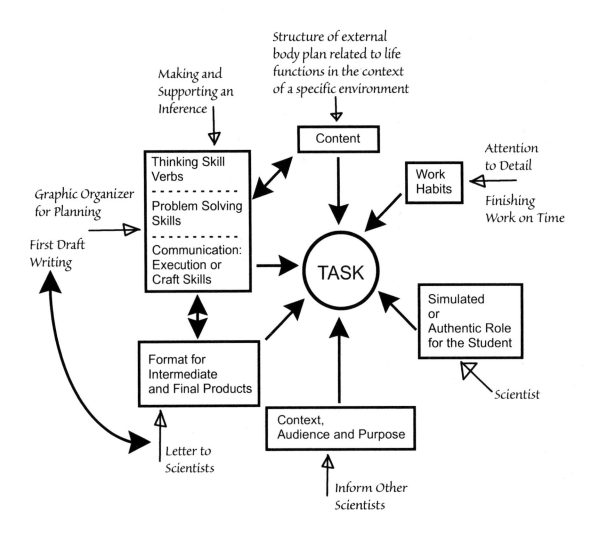

**FIGURE 5.9. PERFORMANCE TASK
SUMMARY FOR DISTRICTWIDE USE**

Performance Task Title: Creature Feature

GRADE LEVEL: **7** DISCIPLINE: **Life Science**	STATE: **CT**

TOPIC: **Surviving in a specific environment**

CONTENT: **Relationship between the structure of living organisms and the functions of those structures**

THEME, ESSENTIAL QUESTION: **How does the environment influence the structures living things have?**

STANDARD: **Know that animals have a great variety of body plans...that serve specific functions for survival.**

THINKING SKILL(S):	FOCUS QUESTIONS CONNECTING CONTENT TO THE THINKING SKILL(S):

Initial Understanding
 	
Developing an Interpretation
    Make and Support an Inference
 	
Making Connections
    Make and Support an Inference
Critical Stance
	What do you think the natural habitat of this creature was?

PROBLEM SOLVING: **Writing Process, including the use of a graphic organizer**

WORK HABIT(S): **Attention to Detail, Finishing Work on Time**

FORMAT OF PRODUCT(S) and/or PERFORMANCE(S): **Written Scientific Explanation with Diagrams**

AUDIENCE: **Scientists**	PURPOSE: **Inform those Scientists**

ROLE OF LEARNER IN THIS TASK: **Scientist**

AUTHOR(S) OF THIS TASK: Mike Hibbard; task adapted from CT State Dept. of Education materials

♦ Thinking Skill Verbs (Fig. 5.2, p. 47)

Now that the outline for the task has been created, the details are completed. One such task is to decide which verb (or verbs) is to be used. The controlling thinking skill verb for the *Creature Feature* task was Inference—"Make and Support an Inference."

♦ Problem-Solving Strategies

Every performance task also connects to one or more problem-solving strategies, such as the writing process, a scientific method, math problem-solving, making models, or inventing. The writing process is the problem-solving strategy used for the *Creature Feature* task. The task requires the student to plan the final product by completing a graphic organizer. This strategy is called prewriting in the overall problem-solving process of writing. (See Appendix C for additional examples of graphic organizers.) Drafting the written response about the *Creature's* natural habitat follows the writing process of thesis statement (the inference) with main ideas and supporting details. The student's skill with the writing process is an important variable in how well that student can show what he or she knows.

♦ Craft Skills

Writing is a common product and much attention is given to the "craft" of writing. But other craft skills are required if the student is asked to construct a model, present an oral presentation, use a computer multimedia program, or illustrate a scientific principle. If the student has not been taught the craft skills relevant to these other formats for final products and performances, that lack of skill may severely limit the student's ability to show what he or she knows. It is incumbent on the teacher to teach the craft skills needed for performance tasks so that eighth grade work does not look like it came from a second grade classroom.

♦ Work Habits

All work requires work habits and for some students, work habits may be the barrier to excellent work. Teachers should review this list of work habits and select one or two on which to focus during a specific performance task:

• Following directions

• Managing time

- Organizing work
- Paying attention to details
- Attending to accuracy
- Collaborating (when appropriate)
- Persisting
- Completing work
- Caring about presentation and neatness
- Self-assessing accurately

TURNING THE PLAN RESULTING FROM THE FRAMEWORK INTO THE PERFORMANCE TASK THAT IS PRESENTED TO THE STUDENT

Figure 2.1 (p. 10) presents the performance task page for *Creature Feature* that the students get. It illustrates that Background, Task, Audience, Purpose, and Procedures are parts of a performance task. The following paragraphs explain what each of task component is intended to do.

Background

The background provides the story line for the performance task. It establishes the reason for the work to be done during the task to make a product or give a performance for a particular audience. The statement of background is an attempt to grab the interest of the students.

Task

The statement of the task simply states what the student is to make or do. The statement of task should be short and to the point, and should not include procedures.

Audience

The audience is identified so that the student can plan how to craft the product or performance to have the desired impact on the audience. Vocabulary and selection of supporting details are two ways to adjust a product or performance to communicate with a specific audience. The *Creature Feature* task asked the students to write to scientists, so using technical vocabulary was appropriate. If the audience were changed to third graders, technical vocabulary would be inappropriate. When the *Creature Feature* task was done without specifying scientists as the audience, many students wrote fantasy stories about the Creature rather than defending a natural habitat for the Creature. When scientists were clearly defined as the audience, most students then approached the task as it was intended.

Purpose

The statement of purpose is also short. It describes the intended impact on the audience, for example, to inform, to explain, to teach, to persuade, to arouse to action, and/or to entertain.

- Some teachers mistakenly think that the Purpose section of a performance task is where to state their purpose or objective for using this task. That is the wrong interpretation of Purpose in the context of this format for a performance task. Purpose, in this context, means the impact that the final product or performance is to have with the audience to whom the student work is directed. In the case of *Creature Feature*, the Purpose of the student's writing and drawing was to inform other scientists about the natural habitat of the Creature.

Procedure

The procedure lists a few directions for the performance task. The fewer directions needed, the better. The procedure should not duplicate items that are stated in the assessment list. For example, if the assessment list has an element that reads, "provide three details to support each main idea," that statement should not also appear in the procedure.

OTHER COMPONENTS OF THE SET OF MATERIALS FOR A PERFORMANCE TASK

The performance task is really a system of materials that includes the task planning form that only teachers see, the performance task, graphic organizers and other materials used for the task, the assessment list, and notes to the teacher.

- Assessment List

   The assessment list for *Creature Feature* is shown in Figure 2.3 (p. 12). Chapter 6 discusses strategies for constructing assessment lists.

- Notes to the Teacher

The set of materials for a performance task include *Notes to the Teacher*. These notes are intended to help the teacher "plan backward" within the unit of instruction called "Structured for Survival." The notes help the teacher pay attention to such things as content, thinking skill verbs, graphic organizers, problem-solving strategies (the writing process for *Creature Feature*), craft skills relevant to the final product (expository writing and drawings for *Creature Feature*), and plans for managing the *Creature Feature* performance task when it is used. These notes are not lesson plans but ideas for shaping lesson plans.

The Notes to the Teacher that follows is provided for the *Creature Feature* task as an example of what the notes could contain. Teachers who use the other tasks in this book, or modifications of them, should construct their own notes based on the resources available to them.

Notes to the Teacher for the *Creature Feature* Task

Following are some suggestions for strategies to focus lessons prior to using the *Creature Feature* performance task.

- ◆ **Content**

  - Review the essential life functions of an organism.

  - Relate the specific structure of external body parts to their roles in carrying out these life functions.

  - During the instruction that precedes *Creature Feature*, look at animals in known environments and see how their body plans are adapted to those environments.

  - Create a bulletin board divided into many different habitats and ask the students to find examples of mammals that live in those habitats. At least one external structure of each animal is to annotated to explain how it is specifically structured to accomplish/ support a life function in that specific habitat.

  - The actual *Creature Feature* task will approach this content from the "other direction." That is, the students will see the *Creature*'s body plan and have to infer the environment. So that it will be novel to the students, don't practice this approach.

◆ **Thinking Skill**

- Making and supporting an inference in the thinking skill to be emphasized.

- Show the students a mouth type or a foot type and have the students infer why that external body part is structured the way it is. Have students use the same type of graphic organizer as in *Creature Feature* to make and support their inference.

◆ **Writing**

- Have the students write a report from the point of view of a scientist informing other scientists. This is a type of expository writing.

- Spend some time showing students examples of grade 7 expository writing in science. Show some examples of excellent work and some examples with flaws, such as lack of clear topic sentence and lack of supporting details.

- Ask the students to work with a partner and use a generic assessment list for writing in science to assess the writing examples you have provided. When they find flaws, the students must explain what could be done to correct those flaws.

SUMMARY

This chapter presents strategies for making performance tasks that are valid because they are connected to curriculum standards, that are user-friendly to the teacher because they are worth the classroom time they take, and that are equitable to the students because they are fair tests of what they know and are able to do. These performance tasks are embedded in classroom instruction to serve as excellent learning activities and opportunities to assess student performance.

Figure 5.1 (p. 42) lists the dimensions of a performance task, and can be used to judge the quality of the performance tasks in this book, those that you find from other sources, and tasks that you create yourself.

Chapter 6 presents strategies for making assessment tools to go with performance tasks.

6

MAKING TOOLS TO ASSESS AND EVALUATE STUDENT WORK

This chapter explains the "function and structure" of an assessment tool and presents strategies for making these assessment tools. To support the use of standards-based embedded performance tasks, assessment tools must provide students and teachers with information that both can use to improve performance. Furthermore, the assessment tools must be easy to make so that all teachers and students will use them.

First, let's define the terms that are used in this chapter.

DEFINITION OF TERMS

Chapter 1 presented six questions that were designed to focus our work on improving student performance. Chapter 4 focused on the question, "What do we want students to know and be able to do?," and Chapter 5 answered the question, "What kinds of tests shall we construct to see how well students perform?"

This chapter addresses three more of the questions posed in Chapter 1:

♦ Question 3: How well should a student perform?

Benchmark or Standard of Performance — A standard of quality against which student work is compared. High goal benchmarks set a high level of expectation for student performance. Sometimes benchmarks come in sets to show what work below the goal looks like, what work at the high goal looks like, and what exceptional work above the high goal looks like.

Benchmarks are also called "anchor papers" or models of student work. Benchmarks can define minimum competence, acceptable levels of performance, and high goals for quality, as well as outstanding work.

Having some benchmarks that define the high goal for student performance and some benchmarks that are purposely flawed so that students can compare and contrast the "good" and the "not so good" as part of understanding the high standards set for them is valuable.

Benchmarks that identify the high goals of student performance help students, teachers, and parents clarify expectations.

We should collect and display benchmarks for at least the most important kinds of student work that our performance tasks call for. If we construct performance tasks that require essays, or three-dimensional models, or plans for scientific experiments, or oral presentations with graphics, or computer-generated products, then we should have benchmarks for those types of products and performances.

When teachers begin to use performance-based learning and assessment they may not have a collection of benchmarks, so their options include:

Making up the benchmarks and then replacing them with real student work as soon as possible.

Using performance tasks without benchmarks first, collecting student work from the use of those tasks, and then identifying the benchmarks to use with subsequent tasks.

Working with colleagues to study student work and select benchmarks is a wonderful way to learn to use student work to improve student performance.

♦ Question 4: How well do students actually perform?

Test (a thing)	An instrument or strategy to collect data on student performance. Tests include the following:

> Multiple Choice
> Short Answer
> Longer Written Response
> Construction Such as a Map or Model
> Oral Presentation
> Actual Work Doing an Experiment
> Lab Notebook

Assessment (a process)	The act of collecting data on the strengths and weaknesses of student performance from the test.
Holistic Assessment	An assessment strategy that defines how well a student does according to a series of categories that define several levels of quality from low to high. The product or performance gets an "overall" score. The assessment tool, called a "holistic rubric," is used for holistic assessment. Rubrics are explained later in this chapter. Figure 6.3 (p. 70) is a holistic rubric.
Analytical Assessment	An assessment strategy that provides data on a number of specific attributes or dimensions of the product or the performance. Each attribute is assessed independently and the product or performance gets a score on each attribute. There are two types of assessment tools usable for analytical assessment. One is an "analytic rubric" and the other is an assessment list. Both are explained later in this chapter. See Figure 6.5 (p. 73) for an analytic rubric and Figures 2.3 (p. 12) and 6.8 (p. 78) for analytic assessment lists.
	The model of performance-based learning and assessment presented in this book uses analytic assessment lists as the assessment tool.
Self-Assessment	The act of using a scoring tool (holistic or analytical) to score one's own product or performance.

Peer Assessment   The act of using a scoring tool (holistic or analytical) to score the product or performance of someone else in your group.

♦ Question 5: To what degree are we satisfied with the quality of our students' actual performance?

Evaluation (a process)   To make an evaluation of student performance is to make a judgment about what the data from assessment means. For example, is it good news or bad news that this particular student's work is somewhat below the high goal set for this work? Figure 6.1 plots the level of student work over time as compared to a high, fixed goal for quality. Bar 1 shows that the student began the year performing at a low level and over the course of the year improved. Arrow B shows how much improvement there was from bar 1 to bar 4. Arrow A shows how much below the high goal the student's best performance still is. Is this student's performance good news or bad news? The teacher's judgment about whether this situation is good news or bad news is an evaluation. In this case, the evaluation should be that this student's improvement is good news even though the performance is still below the high goal set for the performance of seventh graders in this school.

THE PURPOSE AND DESIGN OF AN ASSESSMENT TOOL

This book presents performance assessment as a set of classroom strategies to improve student performance in science. The primary purpose of a scoring tool in this context is to give the teacher and the student the information that they need to improve teaching and learning. A secondary purpose of the scoring tool is to provide information about the quality of the overall science program. There are some issues regarding the design and use of scoring tools that should be considered. They are discussed in the following paragraphs.

VALIDITY AND RELIABILITY

To be valid the assessment tool must address the curriculum standards that form the basis of the performance task. It must be clear through an inspection of the assessment tool what the content, thinking skill, problem-solving, and work

FIGURE 6.1. EVALUATING STUDENT PERFORMANCE

A = Relationship Between Actual Final Performance and High Goal

B = Relationship Between Final Performance and Earlier Performance

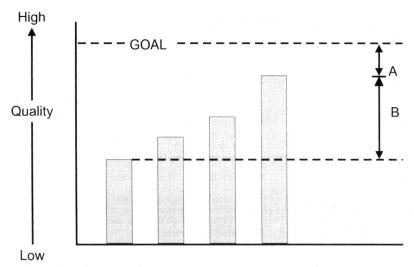

Student Performance on Curriculum Embedded Tasks

Earlier in the Year ──────────► Later in the Year

habit standards are. Often, assessment tools do not attempt to address all curriculum standards relevant to a particular performance task, focusing instead on the most important standards.

To be reliable the assessment tools must give the same results when used repeatedly by the same teacher or different teachers.

SCORING TOOLS SHOULD ALWAYS BE USED IN CONJUNCTION WITH BENCHMARKS

Reliability is greatly enhanced when scoring tools are used in conjunction with benchmarks. Using the assessment tool with benchmarks that have already been assessed helps calibrate the new assessors. Being able to refer to those benchmarks when scoring new samples of student work, improves the reliability of the assessors' work.

SUBJECTIVITY VS. OBJECTIVITY

A legitimate concern about the scoring of work as complex as the student's response to the *Creature Feature* performance task is to what degree the assessment will be objective. It is probably impossible for an assessment of complex work to be completely objective. The goal, then, is to make the assessment as reasonable and justifiable as possible. The tools to accomplish this goal are a scoring tool and a benchmark of student work that shows what the high goal for quality is.

SCORING TOOLS PROVIDE INFORMATION TO IMPROVE PERFORMANCE

The scoring tool needs to give the student specific information about the strengths and weaknesses of his or her products and/or performances. Only with this specific information can a student know what to do to improve his or her performance. The scoring tool needs to give the teacher specific information about the student's performance so that the teacher can adapt materials and strategies that help the student improve his or her performance.

THE ASSESSMENT TOOL SHOULD PROMOTE INDEPENDENT LEARNING

A goal of all teachers is to coach students to be independent learners—to learn the skills and work habits necessary to be lifelong learners. Accurate self-assessment is an essential skill in becoming an independent learner. The scoring tool should promote self-assessment along with assessment by peers, the teacher, and the parents.

THE ASSESSMENT TOOLS SHOULD BE USER-FRIENDLY

The goal is for all teachers and all students to be comfortable making assessment tools that work to guide the improvement of teaching and learning. Thus, the scoring tools should be easy to make and modify for different performance tasks for students with different needs.

DIFFERENT TYPES OF ASSESSMENT TOOLS

This chapter presents options for scoring the student's response to *Creature Feature* that was presented in Chapter 2. Because the format for that final product was a written response supported with sketches, scoring tools for writing are presented in this chapter. Assessment tools presented in Chapter 7 and Appendices A and B are related to many other formats for products and performances.

OPTIONS FOR SCORING TOOLS: THE SCORING TOOL TREE

Figure 6.2 presents the Scoring Tool Tree. Its two branches show that Rubrics and Lists are the two different types of scoring tools explored in this book. Both branches come from a common trunk, which is the Dimension on which all scoring tools for a particular product or performance (in this case writing in science.) The trunk, in turn, grows from the roots, which are:

Authentic Work	Actual writing of this type by real scientists and science writers.
Benchmarks	Samples of this type of writing by students at this grade level and experience. Some benchmarks may come from local, state, and national tests requiring this type of writing.
Curriculum Standards	Language Arts curriculum standards also define what excellent writing should be like.

FIGURE 6.2. SCORING TOOL TREE

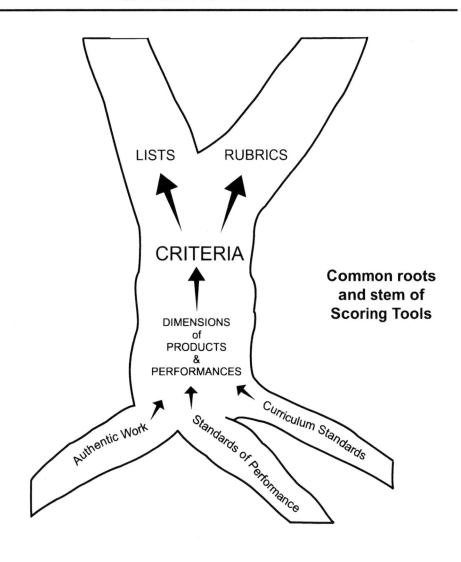

LISTS   RUBRICS

CRITERIA

DIMENSIONS
of
PRODUCTS
&
PERFORMANCES

Common roots
and stem of
Scoring Tools

Authentic Work   Standards of Performance   Curriculum Standards

Below are the dimensions for writing in science that form the trunk of the Scoring Tool Tree. Assessment tools are made from this "trunk of dimensions."

DIMENSIONS OF WRITING IN SCIENCE

Dimension	*Explanation*
Accurate Information	All the information used is scientifically accurate, complete, objective, and appropriate to the topic being written about.
Thinking Skills	The student presents information that has been analyzed by one or more of these processes: sequencing, describing, identifying, comparing, contrasting, inferring, predicting, hypothesizing, identifying cause and effect, judging, assessing, critiquing.
	The analyses used are appropriate to the topic and help show how deeply the student understands the topic. The student makes connections between the current topic and his or her prior knowledge.
Vocabulary	The vocabulary chosen is clear, precise, and appropriate for the science topic and to the audience for the final product. When technical vocabulary is used, it is explained. Sense of audience is an important skill in selecting vocabulary to communicate information and ideas.
Main Ideas	The main ideas are clear, easy to find, accurate, and sufficient in number to fully support the development of the topic.
Details	The supporting details for each main idea are clear, accurate, and sufficient in number to fully support the development of the topic. Supporting details are chosen to support the main ideas and to communicate effectively with the audience for the writing. Again, sense of audience is important.

Dimension	*Explanation*
Organization	The sequence of main ideas in the whole work is a logical response to the topic. The sequence of details supporting a main idea within a paragraph is in a logical order. The writer uses signal words, such as first, next, and finally, to identify the organizational structure of the writing.
Focus	The writer stays on the topic throughout the work and does not bring in extraneous information.
Fluency	The writing is smooth and has a feeling of flow rather than reading as if it were a list. Transition words signal movement from one idea to the next.
Diagrams or Sketches	The diagrams or sketches are on the topic. They are clear, accurate, and labeled. The diagrams show only enough information to support the writing. The diagrams or sketches do not distract from what is being discussed in the writing. Sense of audience helps direct the type of detail of diagrams and sketches.
English Mechanics	The mechanics of English are correct. In a first draft, errors in English do not distract the reader from understanding the writing. In a final draft, there should be no errors.
Neatness and Presentation	The work is neat, presentable, and follows all the format criteria for the assignment.

VISITING THE BRANCHES OF THE SCORING TOOL TREE

First we will visit the Rubric branch of the Scoring Tool Tree and then we will visit the Analytic List branch. Our visit examines how well each type of assessment tool meets the criteria of providing the student and teacher with the specific information that each needs to improve, and how well each type of scoring tool meets the criteria of promoting independent learning on the part of the student.

HOLISTIC RUBRICS

Figure 6.3 is a holistic rubric with seven levels of quality. (Most holistic rubrics have from four to seven levels.) Level 6 is the highest attainable level of performance for a response. Level 0 indicates no response at all. For the holistic rubric in Figure 6.3, each level of the rubric is designated by a numeral rather than a title such as Excellent, Proficient, Good, Poor. Giving titles to the levels of the holistic rubric is an act of Evaluation, a topic that is discussed later in this chapter. For now, the levels of the holistic rubric are designated only by numerals.

FIGURE 6.3. HOLISTIC RUBRIC FOR WRITING IN SCIENCE

Note: These 7 levels are provided as a general guide. Read the student response and then give it a "overall" rating of 6, 5, 4, 3, 2, 1, or 0

- ◆ **SCORE POINT 6: Highest level**
  Well-Developed Responses
  - Main ideas and supporting details are entirely accurate, specific, clear, and sufficient
  - Higher-order thinking highly developed
  - Strong organizational structures throughout
  - Strong use of language throughout
  - Diagrams or sketches are accurate, clear, and focused on the topic

- ◆ **SCORE POINT 5**
  Developed Responses
  - Main ideas and supporting details of the main science concepts are accurate and specific
  - There may be errors in the less important science concepts related to this task
  - Higher-order thinking well developed
  - Organizational structures generally well developed
  - Use of language generally strong
  - Diagrams or sketches help support the writing

- ◆ **SCORE POINT 4**
  Somewhat Developed Responses
  - Main ideas and supporting details are mostly accurate and mostly specific
  - Higher-order thinking developed

- Satisfactory organizational structures
- Language used in a satisfactory manner
- Diagrams or sketches are on the topic

◆ **SCORE POINT 3**

Minimally Developed Responses

- Main ideas mostly accurate but not well supported
- Higher-order thinking somewhat evident
- Some disorganization present
- Language general and not responsive to the specific topic
- Diagrams or sketches present but not helpful in supporting the writing

◆ **SCORE POINT 2**

Undeveloped Response

- Main idea with no support and/or contains major errors in using the main science concepts important to this task
- Very little evidence of higher-order thinking
- Unorganized
- Some language used incorrectly
- Diagrams or sketches are off topic or absent

◆ **SCORE POINT 1**

Sparse Response

- Vague information and/or completely wrong
- Not long enough to have an organization
- No higher-order thinking evident
- Language very immature
- Diagrams and sketches absent

◆ **SCORE POINT 0**

No Response

The purpose of a holistic rubric is to give student work an overall "score." Once a score has been assigned to the student's work, in this case writing in science, a comparison can be made between the quality of the student's current performance and the student's past performances so we can determine whether the student's performance has improved. Another use of the rubric scores is to look at the scores made by all the students in a class or grade level to see what percentage of students are at which levels of the rubric.

The rubric provides some information but it does not tell us about the specific strengths and weaknesses of the student's written responses. Knowing that the student made a score of 4 does not tell the student or the teacher exactly why the student's work is at that level. The student's writing in science may have been assessed at the level of 4 because of a problem with accurate information, insufficient supporting details, or poor organization. Neither the student nor the teacher has enough information from a score from a holistic rubric to know what to do to improve performance.

USING THIS HOLISTIC RUBRIC TO SCORE THE STUDENT RESPONSE TO THE CREATURE FEATURE PERFORMANCE TASK

The student response to the *Creature Feature* task to which the holistic rubric is being applied here is shown in Figure 2.4A on page 13. This student received a holistic score of 5 using this rubric. But why? Maybe it was because higher-order thinking was not highly enough developed throughout the entire paper. Or maybe it was because the examples given were not clear enough? Or was it a problem with the sketches? Without further comment, getting a score of 5 does not help the student know what to do better next time, which is the problem with using a holistic rubric. Neither the student nor the teacher gets specific enough information to help improve his or her teaching and learning.

ANALYTIC RUBRICS

The analytic rubric overcomes the problem of not providing specific enough information. Figure 6.4 presents an analytic rubric for writing in science. Some of the dimensions are listed down the leftmost column. In this case, only six of the dimensions are listed. If all of the dimensions were listed, the analytic rubric would be longer.

The left column lists the six different criteria that we have determined are important for writing in science. Across the top are four columns for different levels of performance. In this case, there are four levels, and the thicker line between levels 2 and 3 indicates that performance at levels 3 and 4 is acceptable, and performance at levels 1 and 2 is unacceptable. We could, then, broadly define the different levels as:

Level 1:   "Very poor," or "Terrible," or "Completely unacceptable"

Level 2:   "Not quite good enough" or "Almost"

Level 3:   "Acceptable" or "Good enough but not great"

Level 4:   "Wonderful," "Exemplary," or "Terrific"

FIGURE 6.4. ANALYTIC RUBRIC FOR WRITING IN SCIENCE

	Level 1 Low	Level 2	Level 3	Level 4 High
Main Ideas				
Supporting Details				
Higher-Order Thinking				
Organization				
Use of Language				
Sketches				

←——— Unacceptable ———→ ←——— Acceptable ———→

In each box we would write descriptions of actual performance that would represent each level for each criterion. For example, for Main Ideas we might decide that a level 1 rating means that the main ideas are not evident; a level 2 rating means that the main ideas are present but not clear; a level 3 rating means that the main ideas are clear and accurate; and a level 4 rating means that the main ideas are clear, accurate, and sufficient in number to completely address the assignment.

The completed analytic rubric in Figure 6.5 can be used to assess the student work found in Figures 2.4A (p. 13) and 2.4B (p. 14). Figure 6.6 applies the analytic rubric of Figure 6.5 to score the student's response.

All of the main ideas that support the inference that the Creature lived in a sandy environment were scientifically logical. Supporting details for each main idea were sufficient and specific. Making and supporting the inference about the natural habitat of the Creature showed the use of higher-order thinking, but this teacher was looking for even more evidence of higher-order thinking. She wanted the students to not only list evidence, but to describe how all the "pieces of evidence" added together to tell a powerful story. That is, she wanted the students to explain how the whole body of evidence was greater than the sum of its parts, but she did not see evidence of this type of higher-order thinking in the student's response.

The teacher did see a high level of organization and an excellent use of vocabulary to present the explanation to the audience of scientists who would read the report. The teacher expected a little more labeling for the sketches that were provided to support the writing.

FIGURE 6.5. AN ANALYTIC RUBRIC ON WRITING IN SCIENCE FOR SCORING THE STUDENT'S RESPONSE TO CREATURE FEATURE

	Level 1 Low	Level 2	Level 3	Level 4 High
Main Ideas	Not present	Present but not clear May include major errors	Clear and accurate May include minor errors	Clear, accurate, and sufficient in number to cover the topic
Supporting Details	Not accurate	Accurate but very sparse May include major errors	Accurate and sufficient in number to support the main ideas May include minor errors	Accurate, sufficient in number, and especially well chosen to support the main ideas
Higher-Order Thinking	Not evident	Somewhat evident	Evident	Strongly evident
Organization	Very unorganized	Somewhat organized	Organized	Strongly organized throughout
Use of Language	Immature use of vocabulary	Vocabulary includes some topic-specific words	Vocabulary includes a good selection of topic-specific words	Vocabulary chosen does an excellent job of addressing both the topic and the audience
Sketches	No sketches	Sketches present but do not support the writing well	Sketches accurate and do support the writing	Sketches accurate and especially clear in supporting the writing

←————Unacceptable————→ | ←———— Acceptable ————→

**FIGURE 6.6. SCORING THE STUDENT RESPONSE
TO THE CREATURE FEATURE PERFORMANCE TASK**

	Level 1 Low	*Level 2*	*Level 3*	*Level 4 High*
Main Ideas				X
Supporting Details				X
Higher-Order Thinking			X	
Organization				X
Use of Language				X
Sketches			X	

←——— *Unacceptable* ——→ ←——— *Acceptable* ——→

COMBINING SCORES ON CRITERIA

Occasionally, it is important to combine scores on different criteria and to arrive at a single score or grade. The next sections describe how to obtain an "overall" score from an analytic rubric.

WEIGHT OF EACH DIMENSION OF THE ANALYTIC RUBRIC

Are all the dimensions of equal importance? Unless one or another is designated as more or less important than the others, they should all be assumed to be of equal importance. Educators should have good reasons for their decisions as to weight, and these discussions can themselves constitute important professional conversations. As an example, we could have determined, in creating the analytic rubric for writing in science, that Main Ideas is the most important dimension, and is worth thrice the value of another dimension, such as organization. Then, our rubric, and the points possible from each dimension, appears as follows:

FIGURE 6.7. ANALYTIC RUBRIC FOR WRITING IN SCIENCE SHOWING WEIGHT FOR EACH DIMENSION

	Level 1 Low	Level 2	Level 3	Level 4 High
Main Ideas weight = 3				3 × 4 = 12
Supporting Details weight = 2				2 × 4 = 12
Higher Order Thinking weight = 2			2 × 3 = 6	
Organization weight = 1				1 × 4 = 4
Use of Language weight = 1				1 × 4 = 4
Sketches weight = 1			1 × 3 = 3	

CALCULATING TOTAL POINTS FROM THE ANALYTIC RUBRIC

How should the scores be calculated? Clearly, the easiest technique is to convert the assigned scores, on each criterion, as reflected in the weights assigned to each criterion, to a percentage of the total possible number of points:

weight × level = criterion score

sum of criterion scores = total score

total score / total possible score = percentage score

The point total for the student's response to the *Creature Feature* performance task is:

Dimension	Weight ×	Level =	Total Score for That Dimension
Main Ideas	3	4	12
Supporting Details	2	4	8
Higher Order Thinking	2	3	6
Organization	1	4	4
Language	1	4	4
Sketches	1	3	3
Total Points Earned			37

On this rubric, the total possible scores for each dimension are:

Main Ideas:	12
Supporting Details:	8
Higher Order Thinking:	8
Organization:	4
Language:	4
Sketches:	4
Total Points Possible:	40

Thus, in our example of a student's response to *Creature Feature*, this student would have received a score of 37, which, when divided by 40 equals 92.5%. A letter grade assigned to this performance would then be an A.

The use of the holistic and analytic rubrics result in similar grades for the student's work on the *Creature Feature* performance task. The analytic rubric provides more information to the student and teacher about the specific strengths and weaknesses of that response. Armed with this more specific information, both the student and teacher know more about what to do to improve teaching and learning.

ACCEPTABLE AND UNACCEPTABLE WORK

Notice that each analytic rubric in this chapter shows that a score of 1 or 2 is unacceptable as a score, and that 3 or 4 is acceptable. This is one way to define the evaluative statements "acceptable" and "unacceptable."

ANALYTIC ASSESSMENT LISTS

Holistic and Analytic Rubrics are two tools for assessing student work. Analytical Lists are another choice. This section describes how to make and use analytic lists that are well-connected to standards, that give the teacher and student the specific information that they need to improve their performance, and that promote self-assessment on the part of the student.

Figure 6.8 presents a generic analytic assessment list for writing in science. The nature of assessment lists is discussed based on this generic assessment list and then several variations of assessment lists for *Creature Feature* are presented and discussed to demonstrate the versatility and "user-friendliness" of analytic assessment lists.

This generic assessment list could be used for a great variety of performance tasks that ask for a written response as the format for the final product. Notice how the elements of this generic assessment list mirror the dimensions of writing discussed earlier on page 68. These generic assessment lists are used with students who have experience with assessment lists much more specifically tailored to the content of the performance task.

FIGURE 6.8. A GENERIC PERFORMANCE TASK ASSESSMENT LIST FOR WRITING IN SCIENCE

Elements	*Assessment Points*		
	Points Possible	*Earned Assessment*	
		Self	*Teacher*
1. The information in the writing and in the diagrams is accurate.		_____	_____
2. The use of thinking skills is clearly evident.		_____	_____
3. The vocabulary used is appropriate to the topic and to the audience.		_____	_____
4. There are enough main ideas to fully develop the topic.		_____	_____
5. There are enough supporting details to explain each main idea.		_____	_____
6. The writing shows strong organization.		_____	_____
7. The writing stays on topic throughout the piece.		_____	_____
8. The response is smoothly written.		_____	_____
9. The drawings or sketches clearly support the information in the writing.		_____	_____
10. The mechanics of English are correct.		_____	_____
11. The work is neat and presentable.		_____	_____
TOTAL:		_____	_____

TAILORED ASSESSMENT LISTS FOR SPECIFIC PERFORMANCE TASKS

Figure 2.3 (p. 12) presents the assessment list tailored for the *Creature Feature* task and the class of student for whom it was intended. Tailored assessment lists respond both to particular aspects of the task and to particular aspects of the students.

Items 1 through 7 of that assessment list are directed at the student's understanding of the scientific principles involved in how animal's body structures allow them to carry out life functions in their specific environments. Each of the seven items on the assessment list gets at a little piece of understanding of the science content. None of these seven elements could stand alone as a measure of how well the students understand the science involved. The teacher wrote those seven items the way that they appear on the assessment list because she thought that having seven items worded in that way would get the students to "pay attention" to the quality of their work. The generic assessment list is not specific enough to "spoon-feed" the answers, but it points the student in the right direction.

Later in this chapter, we will discuss assessment lists for students who are less experienced with performance tasks and assessment lists, and assessment lists for students who are much more experienced with these materials and strategies. We want students to eventually work without assessment tools of any kind.

WHAT KINDS OF ITEMS GO ON THE ASSESSMENT LIST?

When the teacher makes an assessment list, that teacher reviews the dimensions for the kind of work required of students. In the case of the *Creature Feature* assessment list in Figure 2.3 (p. 12), the teacher reviewed the dimensions of writing in science (p. 68) and the generic assessment list for writing in science (Fig. 6.8) to get ideas for what to include in the assessment list tailored for *Creature Feature*.

An analysis the *Creature Feature* assessment list shown in Figure 2.3 indicates that these are the the kinds of elements that were included:

- ◆ Elements 1–7 focus on the science content.

- ◆ Elements 1–3 and 5 also focus on the thinking skill of making and supporting an inference.

- ◆ Element 4 focuses on the thinking skill of explaining how the sum of all the individual pieces of evidence together tell a more powerful story.

- Elements 1–3, 5, and 7–9 focus on writing skills.

- Elements 10 and 11 focus on work habits.

WHY DO ASSESSMENT LISTS INCLUDE ELEMENTS ABOUT WRITING FORMAT AND WORK HABITS?

The quality of someone's work is influenced by what they know (the content), how they think (thinking skills), how well they communicate (writing, speaking, drawing, making, acting out), and how well they employ good work habits. Performance tasks are examples of work that incorporate these four elements. Assessment lists include elements that examine the quality of content knowledge, thinking skills, communication skills, and work habits. The teacher decides how to weave these four elements into the performance task and assessment list, and how much importance to give each.

The sample assessment lists shown in this book include a variety of elements that address writing format issues such as main ideas, supporting details, transition words, use of language, and mechanics of English. There are also work habit elements for skills, such as paying attention to details, organizing work, managing time, working collaboratively, and accurately self-assessing. While important to the overall quality of work, writing format and work habit elements on the assessment lists are not weighted nearly as heavily as elements related to content and thinking skills.

HOW MANY ITEMS GO ON THE ASSESSMENT LIST?

The purpose of the assessment list is to get the student to pay attention to the quality of his or her work and improve his or her performance. So, the assessment list must be long enough to focus the student's attention on as many specific aspects of his or her work as the student will pay attention to. Assessments are usually never more than one page in length. As students develop experience with assessment lists, they gradually are willing to pay attention to an increasing number of items on an assessment list. In September, an assessment list for writing in science may be only have 6 items, but in May, the assessment list for that kind of product may have 12 items. The role of the teacher is to continually stretch the expectations for all students.

HOW ARE POINTS ASSIGNED?

The teacher assigns points to each item in the list to indicate the content and instructional importance of that item. Items 1–3 and 5, which focus on the content of the topic, are worth 60 points. A student cannot do well on this assessment list without knowing the science.

This whole assessment list is worth 100 points, but the teacher could decide that it is worth more or less than 100 points, and then adjust the value of each list item accordingly.

HOW IS THE ASSESSMENT LIST USED?

The assessment list helps students learn to pay attention to the quality of their own work and to improve their performance. The assessment list is given to the students when the performance task is given to them. The assessment list communicates the teacher's expectations clearly. Students study the assessment list before they begin their work, review it as they work, and use it for self-assessment before they submit their work to the teacher. During this self-assessment, students may find ways to improve their performance.

The teacher uses the assessment list to assess both the student's work and the student's self-assessment. The teacher's role includes teaching science and coaching students to take responsibility for their own work. In Figure 2.7 (pp. 16–20), the teacher described how the study of both the student work and student self-assessment resulting from the *Creature Feature* performance task helped her improve her teaching materials and strategies.

USING THE TAILORED ASSESSMENT LIST TO ASSESS AND GRADE THE STUDENT'S RESPONSE TO CREATURE FEATURE

Figure 2.5 (p. 15) shows the student's self-assessment and the teacher's assessment with comments. The student's assessment generally agreed with the teacher's assessment except for item number 4. Figure 2.7 (pp. 16–20) presents the teacher's explanation for the difference between the self-assessment and the teacher's assessment of item 4. The grade is based on the percentage of the total points earned. The student received a grade of A according to this assessment list.

COACHING STUDENTS TO ACCURATELY ASSESS THEIR OWN WORK

The assessment list's purpose is to get students to pay attention to the quality of their work before, during , and at the end of their work, before they hand it in. If self-assessment is inaccurate, the following two strategies often work to improve it. (Figure 2.7, at pages 16–20, presents a full discussion of these two strategies.)

CONVERSATIONS ABOUT BENCHMARKS (MODELS OF STUDENT WORK)

During instruction that comes in the days before the performance task, the teacher presents models of excellent work and an assessment list for them. For example, in preparation for *Creature Feature*, the teacher showed the students examples of written responses to other tasks and together the teacher and class analyzed those examples with their assessment list. The teacher also showed the class purposefully flawed work and asked the students to work in cooperative groups to find the flaws and fix them.

Through these conversations based on the study of criteria and actual student work, the students are "calibrated" so that they know how many points to give themselves during self-assessment. They have learned what the level 10/10 points means as compared, for example, to the level of performance of 6/10 points.

ANNOTATING THE ACTUAL WORK

Teachers hope that when students use assessment lists, they study their work in reference to each item on the assessment list as they are assessing it. When the teacher perceives that the students are not paying strict attention to their work during self-assessment, the teacher may require the students to annotate their work in some way to show how have made the connections between in item on the assessment list and their work. Figures 2.4A (p. 13) and 2.4B (p. 14) show such annotation. The teacher required that the students underline each of the five pieces of evidence required, mark those five pieces E1, E2, and so on, and underline the explanation about how a piece of evidence supported the inference about where the creature lived.

TEACHERS ADD COMMENTS TO ASSESSMENT LISTS

Because the assessment list is made up of specific comments about the specific product or performance of the task, the teacher's scoring of each comment provides specific feedback to the student. But when teachers use the assessment list to assess and grade student work, they often add handwritten notes as shown in Figure 2.5 (p. 15).

ASSESSMENT LISTS ARE DYNAMIC TOOLS FOR GETTING STUDENTS TO PAY ATTENTION

The assessment list is created to be true to the content, thinking skills, problem-solving skills, craft skills, and work habits on which the performance task is based. The assessment list must also be at a level that stretches the student to pay attention to as many of the elements of quality as possible. If the assessment list is too simple or too specific, the student is coddled. If the assessment list is too difficult, the student may feel overwhelmed and ignore it. The teacher's job is to craft the assessment list to encourage, as well as to expect, the students to grow as independent learners doing quality work.

Figures 6.9 and 6.10 are examples of how the assessment list for *Creature Feature* was adapted to meet the needs of two very different students. More than one version of the assessment list can be used in the class at the same time.

WHICH ASSESSMENT LIST IS BEST?

Of the three assessment lists for *Creature Feature* shown in Figures 2.3 (p. 12), 6.9, and 6.10, which is the best to use? The answer is relative to the students for whom the assessment list is intended. For students inexperienced with performance tasks and assessment lists, the assessment list in Figure 6.9 may be more appropriate. For more experienced students, the assessment list in Figure 2.3 may be best, and for even more experienced students, the assessment list in Figure 6.10 may be the match. The most experienced students should not be given any of these three lists; instead, they should work with the class to help make the assessment list for *Creature Feature*.

STUDENTS CAN CREATE THEIR OWN ASSESSMENT LISTS

The goal of using assessment lists is to coach students to become independent learners and to make their own assessment lists on paper, or "in their head," whenever they do work in or out of school. So, besides giving students assessment lists and discussing them in class in conjunction with the use of benchmarks, teachers use these strategies to get students to make assessment lists:

1. The teacher works with the class to create the assessment list, which each student then uses.

2. Students work in cooperative groups of four to make the assessment lists. To make the one assessment list to be used by all students, the teacher uses the lists from all cooperative groups in the class.

3. Students work in pairs to make the assessment list. The teacher reviews each assessment list, and when a list is approved, each member of that pair uses that assessment list for his or her individual work.

4. Students work alone to make the assessment list. All assessment lists are collected and used by the teacher to make the one assessment list to be used by all students.

FIGURE 6.9. ADAPTING THE *CREATURE FEATURE* ASSESSMENT LIST FOR STUDENTS WITH LESS EXPERIENCE AND SKILLS WITH PERFORMANCE TASKS AND ASSESSMENT LISTS

		Assessment Points	
Elements	*Points Possible*	*Earned Assessment*	
		Self	*Teacher*
THE GRAPHIC ORGANIZER			
1. A habitat is identified.	____	____	____
2. Three pieces of supporting evidence are listed.	____	____	____
3. Each piece of evidence is explained.	____	____	____

*****Stop and check the quality of the graphic organize before continuing.********

THE WRITTEN EXPLANATION			
4. The opinion about the habitat of the Creature is clearly stated in paragraph one.	____	____	____
5. Paragraph two gives one piece of evidence to support the opinion.	____	____	____
6. The piece of evidence is explained.	____	____	____
7. Paragraph three gives another piece of evidence to support the opinion.	____	____	____
8. The piece of evidence is explained.	____	____	____
9. Paragraph four gives a final piece of evidence to support the opinion.	____	____	____
10. The piece of evidence is explained.	____	____	____
11. Transition words are used to tie the paragraphs together.	____	____	____
12. Each sentence begins with a capital and ends with a proper punctuation mark.	____	____	____
13. The work was completed on time.	____	____	____
TOTAL:	____	____	____

FIGURE 6.10. ADAPTING THE *CREATURE FEATURE* ASSESSMENT LIST FOR STUDENTS WITH MORE EXPERIENCE AND SKILLS WITH PERFORMANCE TASKS AND ASSESSMENT LISTS

Elements	Points Possible	Assessment Points — Earned Assessment Self	Teacher
1. An opinion as to the natural habitat of the Creature is clearly stated.	___	___	___
2. Five pieces of evidence are listed.	___	___	___
3. For each piece of evidence, you have explained how an observable body structure carries out a specific life function in the environment of the natural habitat you have selected.	___	___	___
4. Evidence includes contrasts and comparisons between the Creature and known animals that live in known habitats.	___	___	___
5. The labeled sketches show the details of the relationship between observable body structures and how they function to carry out specific life functions in that environment.	___	___	___
6. Scientific vocabulary is used.	___	___	___
7. The writing is concise, organized, focused, and flows smoothly from beginning to end.	___	___	___
8. There is agreement between nouns and verbs.	___	___	___
9. Proper letter style is used.	___	___	___
TOTAL:	___	___	___

Note: One point is subtracted for each punctuation and spelling error.

5. Students work alone to make the assessment list. The teacher reviews the list and when it is approved, that student uses the assessment list for his or her own work.

6. Students make assessment lists on their own.

7. Students work from the assessment list "in their heads."

PEER ASSESSMENT

Peer assessment is an important part of performance-based learning and assessment. The *Creature Feature* assessment list does not have a place for peer assessment, but many assessment lists do. Appendix A contains some tasks with assessment lists that include a place for peer assessment.

HOW DO PARENTS REACT TO ASSESSMENT LISTS?

Parents like assessment lists. They find assessment lists easy to understand and appreciate how assessment lists improve communication between the teacher and the student and between the teacher and the parents. Some parents use the assessment lists to check their son or daughter's homework. So, rather than just asking, "Did you do your homework?," the parent can say, "Show me your assessment list and your completed homework," and follow that up with, "Show me the main ideas and three supporting details for each."

SUMMARY

This chapter was about making assessment tools to assess student work on open-ended performance tasks. The purposes of the assessment tool in the context of using performance tasks as embedded learning activities and opportunities to assess student work are:

1. Coaching the student to pay attention to the quality of his or her work.

2. Coaching the student to make and use his or her own assessment lists.

3. Giving the student specific feedback as to the strengths and weaknesses of his or her work so that the student can make and work toward improving his or her performance.

4. Giving the teacher specific feedback as to the strengths and weaknesses of the students' work so that the teacher can plan and work toward adapting teaching materials and strategies to improve student performance.

7

PERFORMANCE TASKS FOR A SCIENTIFIC METHOD

This chapter addresses the performance tasks for a scientific method from these three perspectives:

1. How well can the student design, carry out, and analyze experiments?

2. How well can the student use a scientific method for consumer decision-making?

3. How well can the student critique another person's use of the scientific method?

DIMENSIONS OF A SCIENTIFIC PROCESS

Before we visit performance tasks that address the scientific method, we must have a definition of a scientific method. Figure 7.1 presents the dimensions of the problem-solving process called a *scientific process* or a *scientific method*. Its overall components are Understanding the Problem, Planning the Experiment, Carrying Out the Experiment, and Communicating the Results Through a Final Report. These categories and their specific dimensions are intended to be a guideline for teachers making performance tasks. No single list can define the highly complex, variable set of strategies called a scientific process. No single performance task should include all of these dimensions, but over the course of the school year, all of these dimensions should be covered. Specific performance tasks and assessment lists show which dimensions the teacher selected as the focus for learning and assessment.

FIGURE 7.1. A SCIENTIFIC PROCESS—MIDDLE SCHOOL

UNDERSTANDING THE PROBLEM, the student:

1. Makes observations.

2. Identifies a topic for an experiment.

3. Asks questions such as, "What happens when I _____?"

4. Works with the class to discuss the audience for the final report and how that report should be constructed to be meaningful to that audience.

PLANNING THE EXPERIMENT, the student:

1. Identifies the issue or problem.

2. Asks a question that will be the basis for the experiment.

3. Finds information from print or electronic sources about the question or the problem.

4. Makes a guess or states a hypothesis about the problem to be solved.

5. Plans the experiment to answer the question.

6. Works with the class to talk about only changing one thing at a time. (Manipulating one independent variable at a time.) Individually selects the independent variable to be changed.

7. Works with the class to list what will remain the same so that there will be a "fair test" of the one thing (independent variable) changed.

8. Works with the class to decide on what will be measured to determine the results of the experiment. (Selecting the dependent variable(s).) Individually selects the dependent variable to be measured.

9. Plans how to repeat the experiment. Talks about how doing the experiment more than one time helps the experimenter have more confidence in the results.

10. Talks with the class about what a "control" is. Individually plans for controls.

11. Plans how to make the measurements and collect the data.

12. Plans how to organize the data collected.

13. Works with the class to talk about how to reduce errors.

14. Works with the class to talk about and plan safe procedures.

15. Works with the class to make assessment lists that will be used to judge the quality of the work done during the experiment.

16. Uses models of excellent work and models with flaws to understand more about what quality looks like.

CARRYING OUT THE EXPERIMENT, the student:

1. Uses safe procedures.

2. Participates in "hands-on" activities.

3. Makes observations.

4. Uses metric and nonmetric scales and tools to measure size, weight, and volume, but the student must learn which levels of specification are appropriate for the case in question:

   Length to the nearest ⅛–inch and nearest millimeter
   Weight to the pound and ounce, kilogram and gram
   Volume to cubic inches or cubic centimeters
   Capacity to the quart, gallon, or liter
   Time to the minute and second
   Temperature to the nearest degree Celsius and Fahrenheit

5. Measures other attributes, such as pH, hardness, and density, and concentration of chemicals, such as oxygen, nitrogen, phosphorous, and potassium.

6. Invents strategies, tools, and scales to make qualitative measurements to measure the physical attributes of objects when no quantitative scale or tool is available.

7. When a tool is invented, the tool is calibrated thus creating a "standardized" way of measuring a physical attribute of an object.

8. Follows directions involving hands-on activities.

9. Follows procedures involving collecting data.

10. Draws pictures to record observations.

11. Describes the range of the data collected.

12. Calculates the mean, mode, and median when appropriate.

13. Makes charts and tables to organize data.

14. Makes line, bar, circle, and picture graphs as appropriate for the data. Some students may use box and whisker graphs. By Grade 7, students should know what kinds of data are appropriate and inappropriate for a line graph. (See the criteria for making graphs in Grade 7.)

COMMUNICATING THE RESULTS THROUGH A FINAL REPORT, the student:

1. Uses an assessment list to guide and self-assess work on a final product that can include drawing, writing, graphs, and 3-D models.

2. Uses models of excellent work and models with flaws to understand more about what quality looks like.

3. Writes according to the expectations for Grade 7 Expository Writing.

4. On some occasions, the data from the experiment is used to support a position. In these cases, the student writes according to the expectations for Grade 7 Persuasive Writing.

5. Uses quantitative language of measurement.

6. Uses language of qualitative measurement such as some, more, most, some, less, least, faster, slower, the same as, and equal to.

7. Uses this quantitative or qualitative language to specifically describe rates of change when that is appropriate to the experiment.

8. Sometimes constructs models to help communicate what the experiment was about.

9. Restates the purpose for the experiment.

10. Summarizes the procedures used.

11. Organizes the data. Makes titles and labels.

12. Makes line, bar, circle, or picture graphs appropriate for both the data and the audience. Some students may use box and whisker graphs.

13. Some students may begin to make and use formulas to describe the rates of change shown on the graphs.

14. States either a conclusion or an answer to the original question.

15. Backs up either the conclusion or the answer by pointing to data including that which is displayed on the graph.

16. Extrapolates and/or predicts from the data displayed on the graph.

17. Evaluates the original guess or hypothesis.

18. Works with the class to talk about errors that may have occurred. Begins organizing the types of errors into categories. Expands the discussion on how to reduce error, noting that errors can never be eliminated entirely.

19. Works with the class to judge how well the experiment was carried out.

20. Talks with the class about "how much confidence" one should place in these results based on the discussion about experimental design and errors.

21. Critiques the experimental procedures done by other experimenters. The teacher supplies excellent and flawed models of experiments carried out by other students. These seventh graders identify strengths and flaws in experimental design and conclusions drawn based on data from those experiments. When flaws are found, ideas for fixing them are discussed. Coach students to use the dimensions of scientific process as the framework through which to view the experimental design of others.

22. Asks followup questions that could lead to further experiments.

PERFORMANCE TASKS THAT INCLUDE BOTH THE SCIENTIFIC METHOD AND SCIENCE CONTENT

Figure 7.2 presents the *Salt on Ice Experiment* performance task, which asks the student to do an experiment about the relationship between the type of salt (size of the salt crystals) and how fast ice melts. Figure 7.3 provides the steps to be followed because the students are not experienced enough (not performance-mature enough) with the scientific method to design their own experiments yet. Figures 7.4 (p. 94) and 7.5 (p. 95) are the blank data table and graphs that the students will use. Figure 7.6 (p. 96) is the assessment list to assess the student's work filling in the data table and putting that data on the graph. When students are more performance-mature, they will be expected to design their own data tables and graphs.

FIGURE 7.2. SALT ON ICE

Background

People who live where there is ice on the roads and sidewalks in the winter apply salt or some other chemical to that ice so that they can travel safely.

Susan woke up one morning and saw that there was a sheet of ice on her driveway. When she went to the garage to get the special ice-thawing chemical that she had bought at the hardware store, she discovered that it was all gone. Susan remembered that she had salt in her kitchen. In her kitchen, she found two kinds of salt. One kind was large crystals of sea salt and the other kind was regular table salt that was made of tiny crystals. She wondered, "Which kind of salt will melt the ice better?"

Task

Your job is to determine which kind of salt does a better job of melting ice. You will write a one-paragraph explanation of which type of salt works best and why it works best.

Audience

You will write your explanation to Susan.

Purpose

Susan always wants to know how things work, so she wants you to explain your conclusion about which salt is best to use to melt the ice.

Procedure

1. Study the assessment list for *Salt on Ice* Data Chart and Graph.

2. Study the assessment list for *Salt on Ice* Explanation to Susan.

3. Carry out the experiment.

4. Collect and display the data.

5. Write your explanation to Susan.

FIGURE 7.3. SALT ON ICE EXPERIMENT

Hypothesis
The size of the salt crystals will influence the rate at which the ice melts.

Prediction
Large-crystal salt will do a better job of melting ice than small-crystal salt.

Materials
1. Two 12-ounce clear-plastic glasses
2. Two 100-cc graduated cylinders
3. A clock or watch with a second hand
4. A small paper nut cup full of large-crystal salt (full to the top but not mounded)
5. Another small paper nut cup full of small-crystal salt (full to the top but not mounded)
6. Ice

   It is best if the ice is in the form of tiny cubes about ½-inch square. These ice cubes must not be stuck together in big masses. Crushed ice will do as long as all the pieces are small, about the same size, and not stuck together in big chunks.

Experimental Procedure
1. Fill each plastic glass right to the top (not mounded up) with ice so that each plastic glass has the same amount of ice in it.
   Keep big chunks or masses of ice out of the plastic glasses.
2. Mark one plastic glass LARGE-CRYSTAL SALT and the other plastic glass SMALL-CRYSTAL SALT.
3. Mark one graduated cylinder "Water From Large-Crystal Salt Plastic Glass" and mark the other graduated cylinder "Water From Small-Crystal Salt Plastic Glass."
4. Pour the large-crystal salt on the ice in the LARGE-CRYSTAL SALT plastic glass. Scatter the salt evenly over the top surface of the ice in that plastic glass.
5. Pour the small-crystal salt on the ice in the SMALL-CRYSTAL SALT plastic glass. Scatter the salt evenly over the top surface of the ice in that plastic glass.
6. Every 3 minutes for 21 minutes make these observations:
   Measure the amount of liquid water in each plastic glass.
   Record the data in the data chart.
7. Put the data into a graph.

Analysis and Conclusion
1. Was the original hypothesis correct or wrong? Use the data to support your opinion of the original hypothesis.
2. What is the science behind what happened to the ice in the two plastic glasses?
3. Write your explanation to Susan. Use the graph in your letter to her.

FIGURE 7.4. DATA CHART

Title of Data Chart	

Length of Time Salt is on Ice	Amount of Melt Water in Milliliters			
	Type of Salt		Type of Salt	
	Amount of Water	Units of Measurement	Amount of Water	Units of Measurement

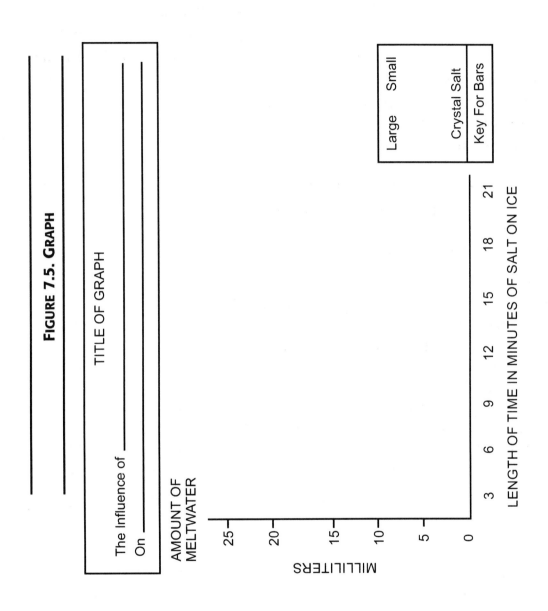

FIGURE 7.5. GRAPH

FIGURE 7.6. PERFORMANCE TASK ASSESSMENT LIST
DATA CHART AND GRAPH—SALT ON ICE EXPERIMENT

Elements	Points Possible	Self	Teacher
		Assessment Points	
		Earned Assessment	
THE DATA CHART			
1. The title given to the data chart explains what the data chart is about.	____	____	____
2. Data for time are recorded and the units are shown.	____	____	____
3. The "Type of Salt" label is completed.	____	____	____
4. Data for amount of water are recorded and units are shown.	____	____	____
5. All data entries are legible.	____	____	____
THE GRAPH			
6. The title given to the graph explains what the graph is about.	____	____	____
7. The bars for the data from the large-crystal salt are shown for each time.	____	____	____
8. The bars for the data from the small-crystal salt are shown or each time.	____	____	____
9. All bars are accurate according to the data in the data chart.	____	____	____
10. All bars are drawn neatly.	____	____	____
TOTAL:	____	____	____

Because this performance task focuses on both the process of using the scientific method and the science concepts involved, the students are required to explain why one type of salt melts the ice faster than the other. The assessment list in Figure 7.7 is for this written explanation, which is in the form of a letter to Susan. Items 2 through 6 focus on the content and can be weighted to emphasize a focus on understanding the science content of the *Salt on Ice Experiment*.

CONSUMER RESEARCH AS AN AUTHENTIC APPLICATION OF THE SCIENTIFIC METHOD

An authentic performance task is one in which the work done, and the product and/or performances made, are similar to the ones that really occur in the student's world. The student may find little need to use what is seen as the "school version" of the scientific method, but may find a use for the application of that problem-solving strategy in the area of consumer decision-making. Figure 7.8 (p. 99) presents a performance task called *Consumer Newsletter Project* that involves both individual and group work in researching consumer products and publishing a consumer newsletter. Figure 7.9 (p. 101) is the assessment list for the whole process, from planning the fair test, to carrying out the fair test, to communicating the findings in a consumer newsletter. This particular performance task is designed for students who have considerable experience with the scientific method. More structure has to be built into this performance task if it is to be used with less performance-mature students.

This project can result in real consumer newsletters that go to real people in the school and/or the community. Consumer research versions of the scientific method are well connected to the standards of a science curriculum and are also engaging to students. An interested student is a hard-working student. A hard-working student is one who improves his or her performance and feels even more capable of doing better next time.

THE SCIENCE FAIR

Science fairs are opportunities for students to have authentic audiences for their work with the scientific method. The work students do along the way—planning an experiment, running it and collecting data, analyzing the data and reaching conclusions, and putting together reports and displays—can be assessed one step at time with assessment lists for each of those steps.

The final project and its display can be assessed with a user-friendly assessment list that can be used by the judges, the students, the teacher, and the parents. Figure 7.10 (p. 104) is an analytic rubric for assessing a science fair entry's quality. Each element is a summary of a much more specific assessment list used during the development phase of the science fair project. This is a good example of how assessment lists and analytic rubrics complement each other.

FIGURE 7.7. PERFORMANCE TASK ASSESSMENT LIST WRITTEN EXPLANATION OF THE SCIENCE BEHIND THE SALT ON ICE EXPERIMENT

Letter to Susan

Elements	Points Possible	Earned Assessment	
		Self	Teacher
1. There is a short summary statement of which type of salt melts ice faster.	_____	_____	_____
2. A simplified version of the graph is included to show which type of salt melts ice faster.	_____	_____	_____
3. The explanation includes a description of how salt melts ice.	_____	_____	_____
4. The explanation includes a description of why one type of salt does a better job of melting the ice than the other kind of salt.	_____	_____	_____
5. Diagrams may be used to help make the explanations clearer.	_____	_____	_____
6. Technical vocabulary is used and explained.	_____	_____	_____
7. This is first draft writing but the spelling is good enough to not distract the reader.	_____	_____	_____
TOTAL:	_____	_____	_____

Figure 7.8. CONSUMER NEWSLETTER PROJECT

Background

Every day people make decisions about how to spend their money on consumer products such as paper towels, laundry detergent, or car wax. They are concerned about getting a good deal and worry that they might not be spending their money wisely. Consumer advocates do research and provide information to consumers to help them make those decisions.

You have been hired by the *Consumer Watchdog Newsletter* to be a part of its consumer products research team.

Task

Your task is to decide on a consumer product to test and to use the scientific method to design and do a test of that product.

You will write your findings in an article for the *Consumer Watchdog Newsletter.*

Audience

Your audience is those people who read the newsletter.

Purpose

The purpose of your work is to inform consumers in an accurate and honest way of the quality of a consumer product.

Procedure

Please read the material for the entire packet before you begin any work.

Group Work

1. Review the assessment lists for Group Work.
2. You will be working as a team of four. Each of you will select and test a separate product.
3. Decide what four consumer products your group will test. Select consumer products that you can test in the classroom or on school property. All testing will be done in school.
4. Decide which person in your group will test which product.
5. The group will make a time and task management plan for the group parts of this project.

(Continued on next page.)

6.   When the entire project is over each person in the group will use the Group Work assessment list to assess the quality of the group work.

Individual Work

7.   Study the assessment list for "Critiquing a Consumer Research Project."

8.   Make a time and task management plan for your individual work.

9.   Design a "fair test" for the consumer product that you selected. This "fair test" is the consumer research version of the scientific method.

Note: Get your "fair test" plan approved by the teacher before you begin to make this "fair test."

10.   Collect data and organize that data in data charts.

11.   Select graphs that are appropriate for the kind of data you have collected and that are interesting to the readers of the *Consumer Watchdog Newsletter.*

12.   Review samples of consumer newsletters to see the writing style used in those kinds of publications.

13.   Write your consumer newsletter article.

14.   Your assessment and your grade will be based on your part of this project.

Group Work

15.   Now your group will put all four of the consumer articles into one newsletter. These newsletters are similar to those that we have done previously in class this year.

16.   Plan the layout of this newsletter.

17.   Make the newsletter.

18.   Give the newsletter to people who will actually use it to think about what they buy.

FIGURE 7.9. CRITIQUING CONSUMER RESEARCH

	Rating			
Dimension	*High*	*Medium*	*Low*	*Very Low*

PLANNING THE FAIR TEST, THE RESEARCHER:

	High	Medium	Low	Very Low
1. States what consumer product is to be tested.	_____	_____	_____	_____
2. Identifies characteristics of the consumer product that are important to the consumer.	_____	_____	_____	_____
3. Selects which characteristics of the consumer product are to be tested.	_____	_____	_____	_____
4. Plans how each characteristic will be tested in a fair way.	_____	_____	_____	_____
5. Plans strategies to control variables.	_____	_____	_____	_____
6. Plans for multiple trails.	_____	_____	_____	_____
7. Plans strategies to reduce error.	_____	_____	_____	_____
8. Plans strategies to use safe procedures.	_____	_____	_____	_____
9. Plans data organization strategies.	_____	_____	_____	_____

CARRYING OUT THE FAIR TEST, THE RESEARCHER:

	High	Medium	Low	Very Low
10. Carries out the planned procedure.	_____	_____	_____	_____
11. Uses safe procedures.	_____	_____	_____	_____
12. Collects data.	_____	_____	_____	_____
13. Organizes data.	_____	_____	_____	_____
14. Processes and analyzes data using appropriate statistical and other mathematical procedures.	_____	_____	_____	_____

(Figure continues on next page.)

		Rating		
Dimension	*High*	*Medium*	*Low*	*Very Low*

COMMUNICATING THE RESULTS THROUGH A CONSUMER NEWS-LETTER: THE RESEARCHER

15. Identifies the product on which the report is about.	_____	_____	_____	_____
16. Provides the researcher's name.	_____	_____	_____	_____
17. Summarizes the purpose for the consumer product study.	_____	_____	_____	_____
18. Summarizes the procedures used.	_____	_____	_____	_____
19. Displays data and its analysis.	_____	_____	_____	_____
20. Uses graphs that are appropriate for the type of data and are also interesting to the reader.	_____	_____	_____	_____
21. Uses illustrations effectively.	_____	_____	_____	_____
22. States a conclusion that is strongly supported by the data.	_____	_____	_____	_____
23. Asks follow-up questions that may lead to further study.	_____	_____	_____	_____
24. Is written in a clear, concise, and straightforward tone.	_____	_____	_____	_____
25. Everyday vocabulary is used.	_____	_____	_____	_____
26. The mechanics of English are correct.	_____	_____	_____	_____
27. The overall layout of the article makes it easy to read.	_____	_____	_____	_____

****

The overall strengths are:

The overall weaknesses are:

Another tool for assessing the quality of the design, execution, and report of an experiment is the assessment list in Figure 7.11. This list can be made shorter and/or the wording of specific elements can be tailored to specific experiments. This assessment list and the rubric in Figure 7.10 can be used by the student and anyone else who judges the quality of the experiment.

When the students have enough experience with rubrics and/or assessment lists for parts of or all of the scientific method, the teacher should then involve them in helping to make assessment tools for their performance tasks. In this way, the students feel more committed to paying attention to the quality of their work and they better understand the judge's reaction to their science fair project.

SUMMARY

Chapter 7 presented performance tasks that ask students to use a scientific method and apply it to the everyday process of consumer decision-making.

FIGURE 7.10. ANALYTIC RUBRIC FOR THE SCIENCE FAIR

	Level 1 Low	Level 2	Level 3	Level 4 High
Experimental Design weight = 3	Most elements of an experimental design are missing and/or there are many serious mistakes.	Most elements of an experimental design are present but there may be some minor mistakes in their use.	All important elements of experimental design are present and correctly used.	All elements of an experiment are clearly evident and used correctly.
Data Analysis weight = 2	Data not analyzed or analyzed extremely poorly.	Data are analyzed but not completely. There may be substantial errors in the use of math and statistics.	Data are analyzed using appropriate math and statistics. There may be minor errors.	Data are analyzed accurately using appropriate math including statistics.
Data Presentation weight = 2	Data charts and graphs are of poor quality if present at all.	Data charts and graphs are marginal in quality.	Data charts and graphs are well done.	Data charts and graphs are perfectly done.
Science Content weight = 3	Science content is inaccurate and/or very incomplete.	There are some errors or omissions in the application of the science content.	The science content is accurate.	The science information is accurate and shows insight into the content.
Craft Skills weight = 1	Work shows poor level of craft skills.	Work shows marginal level of craft skills.	Work shows good level of craft skills.	All work shows very high level of craft skills.
Overall Impact on the Viewer weight = 2	The whole display is confusing to view.	The whole display seems a bit confusing. It does not grab your attention very strongly.	The whole display is interesting and easy to understand.	The whole display is very interesting and easy to understand. It really grabs your attention.

FIGURE 7.11. CRITIQUING A SCIENTIFIC EXPERIMENT

	Rating			
Dimension	*High*	*Medium*	*Low*	*Very Low*
PLANNING THE EXPERIMENT, THE RESEARCHER:				
1. States an hypothesis.	____	____	____	____
2. Identifies (an) independent variable(s) relevant to the hypothesis.	____	____	____	____
3. Identifies (a) dependent variable(s) relevant to the hypothesis.	____	____	____	____
4. Selects an independent variable to use and a dependent variable to measure.	____	____	____	____
5. Predicts the relationship between the independent and dependent variables.	____	____	____	____
6. Plans strategies to control variables.	____	____	____	____
7. Plans controls.	____	____	____	____
8. Plans for multiple trails.	____	____	____	____
9. Plans strategies to reduce error.	____	____	____	____
10. Plans strategies to use safe procedures.	____	____	____	____
11. Plans data organization strategies.	____	____	____	____
CARRYING OUT THE EXPERIMENT, THE RESEARCHER:				
12. Carries out the planned procedure.	____	____	____	____
13. Uses safe procedures.	____	____	____	____
14. Collects data.	____	____	____	____
15. Organizes data.	____	____	____	____
16. Processes and analyzes data using appropriate statistical and other mathematical procedures.	____	____	____	____

(Figure continues on next page.)

		Rating		
Dimension	*High*	*Medium*	*Low*	*Very Low*

COMMUNICATING THE RESULTS THROUGH A FINAL REPORT, THE RESEARCHER:

	High	Medium	Low	Very Low
17. Summarizes the purpose for the experiment.	_____	_____	_____	_____
18. Summarizes the procedures used.	_____	_____	_____	_____
19. Displays data and its analysis.	_____	_____	_____	_____
20. Uses graphics effectively.	_____	_____	_____	_____
21. Evaluates the hypothesis.	_____	_____	_____	_____
22. Generalizes or extrapolates from the data according to the interests of the audience.	_____	_____	_____	_____
23. Critiques the quality of the experimental design and the work to carry out the experiment.	_____	_____	_____	_____
24. Asks follow-up questions that may lead to further experiments.	_____	_____	_____	_____

APPENDIX A

PERFORMANCE TASKS

INDEX OF PERFORMANCE TASKS

Note: All standards and benchmarks for the tasks in this book come from John S. Kendall and Robert J. Marzano, *Content Knowledge: A Compendium of Standards for K-12 Education*, 2nd ed., Aurora, CO: Mid-continent Regional Educational Laboratory (McRel), 1997.

CURRICULUM STANDARDS FOR PERFORMANCE TASKS

Action and Reaction Poster Performance Task

Science Standard 12:

- Understands motion and the principles that explain it.
  - *Benchmark:* Knows that laws of motion can be used to determine the effects of forces on the motion of objects (e.g.,... Whenever one object exerts force on another, a force equal in magnitude and opposite in direction is exerted on the first object.)

Deer Dilemma Performance Task

Science Standard 7:

- Understands how species depend on one another and on the environment for survival.
  - *Benchmark:* Knows factors that affect the number and types of organisms an ecosystem can support (e.g., available resources; abiotic factors such as quantity of light and water, ranges of temperatures, and soil composition; disease; competition from other organisms within the ecosystem, predation).

Electric Circuits Performance Task

Science Standard II:

- Understands energy types and conversions, and their relationship to heat and temperature.
  - *Benchmark:* Knows that electrical circuits provide a means of transferring electrical energy to produce (transform into) heat, light, sound and chemical changes.

Electric Energy Transformation and Transfer

Science Standard II:

- Understands energy types and conversions, and their relationship to heat and temperature.
  - *Benchmark:* Knows that electrical circuits provide a means of transferring electrical energy to produce (transform into) heat, light, sound and chemical changes.

Forensic Scientist Performance Task

Science Standard 15:

- Understands the nature of scientific inquiry.
  - *Benchmark:* Establishes relationships based on evidence and logical argument.

Math Standard 6:

- Understands and applies basic and advanced concepts of statistics and data analysis.
  - *Benchmark:* Understands the basic characteristics of measures of central tendency (e.g., mean, mode, median).

Heartbeat Performance Task

Science Standard 15:

- Understands the nature of scientific inquiry.
  - *Benchmark:* Designs and conducts a scientific investigation (e.g., formulates questions, designs and executes investigations, interprets data, synthesizes evidence into explanations for observations, critiques explanations and procedures).

Insect Mouth Parts Performance Task

Science Standard 4:

- Knows about the diversity and unity that characterize life.
  - *Benchmark:* Knows that animals and plants have a great variety of body plans and internal structures that serve specific functions for survival.

Invent a Musical Instrument Performance Task

Science Standard 12:

- Understands motion and principles that explain it.
  - *Benchmark:* Knows that vibrations (e.g., sounds, earthquakes) move at different speeds in different materials, have different wavelengths, and set-up wave-like disturbances that spread away from the source.

Technology Standard 4:

- Understands the nature of technological design.
  - *Benchmark:* Designs a solution or product, taking into account needs and constraints (e.g., cost, time, trade-offs, properties of materials, safety, aesthetics).

Invent a Worm Farm for Making Soil Performance Task

Science Standard 7:

- Understands how species depend on one another and on the environment for survival.
  - *Benchmark:* Knows factors that affect the number and types of organisms an ecosystem can support (e.g., available resources, abiotic factors such as quantity of light and water, range of temperatures, and soil composition; disease; competition from other organisms within the ecosystem; predation).

Technology Standard 4:

- Understands the nature of technology design.
    - *Benchmark:* Designs a solution or product, taking into account needs and constraints (e.g., cost, time, trade-offs, properties of materials, safety, aesthetics).

Local Watershed Map Performance Task

Geography Standard 1:

- Understands the characteristics and uses of maps, globes, and other geographic tools and technologies.
    - *Benchmark:* Transforms primary data into maps, graphs, and charts.

Geographic Standard 3:

- Understands the characteristics and uses of spatial organization of the Earth's surface.
    - *Benchmark:* Understands patters of land use in urban, suburban, and rural areas.

Machine Skit Performance Task

Technology Standard 5:

- Understands the nature and operations of systems.
    - *Benchmark:* Knows that a system can include processes as well as components.
    - *Benchmark:* Identifies the elements, structure, sequence, operation, and control of a system.

Model of an How an Enzyme Works Performance Task

Science Standard 6:

- Knows the general structure and function of cells in organisms.
    - *Benchmark:* Understands the chemical reactions involved in cell functions (e.g., food molecules taken into cells are broken down to provide the chemical constituents needed to synthesize other molecules; enzymes facilitate the breakdown and synthesis of molecules).

Rock Cycle Performance Task

Science Standard 2:

- Understands basic Earth processes.
    - *Benchmark:* Knows processes involved in the rock cycle (e.g., old rocks at the surface gradually weather and form sediments that are buried, then compacted, heated, and often recrystallized into new rock; this rock is eventually brought to

the surface by the forces that drive plate motions, and the rock cycles continues).

Rolling Down the River Performance Task

Science Standard 2:

- Understanding basic Earth processes.
  - *Benchmark:* Knows how land forms are created through a combination of constructive forces such as crustal deformation, volcanic eruptions, and deposition of sediment and destructive forces such as weathering and erosion.

States of Matter Skit Performance Task

Science Standard 10:

- Understands basic concepts about the structure and properties of matter.
  - *Benchmark:* Knows that atoms are in constant motion (atoms in solids are close together and don't move about easily; atoms in liquids are close together but move about easily; atoms in gas are quite far apart and move around freely).

What Do You Eat? Performance Task

Health Standard 6:

- Understands essential concepts about nutrition and health.
  - *Benchmark:* Classifies food and food combinations into groups.

Math Standard 6:

- Understands and applies basic and advanced concepts of statistics and data analysis.
  - *Benchmark:* Organizes and displays data using tables, graphs, frequency distributions, and plots.

Worm Project Performance Task

Science Standard 2:

- Understands basic Earth processes
  - *Benchmark:* Knows components of soil and other factors that influence soil texture, fertility, and resistance to erosion (e.g., plant roots and debris, bacteria, worms, rodents).

Science Standard 4:

- Knows about the diversity and unity that characterizes life.
  - *Benchmark:* Knows that animals and plants have a great variety of body plans and internal structures that serve specific functions for survival.

Science Standard 7:

- Understands how species depend on one another and on the environment for survival.
    - *Benchmark:* Knows relationships that exist among organisms in food chains and food webs.

ACTION AND REACTION POSTER
PERFORMANCE TASK

Background

One of the big ideas in physics is "For Every Action There Is an Equal and Opposite Reaction." What does this big idea mean? Do people experience this "physics" in their everyday lives?

Task

Your task is find examples of this big idea in physics that occur in your everyday life.

You will then make a creative, interesting, and scientifically accurate poster to show how "for every action there is an equal and opposite reaction" really does occur in everyday life.

Audience

Accurate posters will be displayed in the town library.

Purpose

The purpose of your poster is to explain science to citizens.

Procedure

1. Review the assessment list for this task.

2. Make a plan for your poster.

PERFORMANCE TASK ASSESSMENT LIST
ACTION AND REACTION POSTER

Elements	Points Possible	Earned Assessment Self	Teacher
1. The poster has an interesting title.	____	____	____
2. The picture is an accurate way to show the physics concept: "For Every Action There Is an Equal and Opposite Reaction."	____	____	____
3. The picture is a creative and interesting way to show the physics concept: "For Every Action There Is an Equal and Opposite Reaction."	____	____	____
4. Arrows are used to show the forces of action and reaction.	____	____	____
5. Labels and very short statements are used to explain the actions and reactions shown in the picture.	____	____	____
6. The whole poster can be viewed and understood in about 20 seconds by someone who knows no science.	____	____	____
TOTAL:	____	____	____

DEER DILEMMA
PERFORMANCE TASK

Background

The Commissioner of Parks in your State has decided that there are too many deer in the State's parks. She is considering a plan to allow a certain number of deer to be killed so that the deer population will be reduced. What is your opinion of this plan?

Task

Your task is to decide whether you support the Commissioner's plan to allow deer to be killed in Putnam Park and to write a letter persuading her about your opinion.

Audience

The Commissioner of Parks is your audience.

Purpose

The purpose of your letter is to persuade the Commissioner to follow your advice.

Procedure

1. Read the assessment list for the Deer Dilemma Persuasive Letter.

2. Make and use your own graphic organizer to plan your letter.

3. Write a first draft of your letter.

4. Use the assessment list to assess your letter and get a peer to assess your work.

5. Make revisions as indicated by your self-assessment and the assessment you got from your peer assessor.

6. Write a final draft.

7. Use the assessment list to make your final assessment and turn in the letter along with your self-assessment.

PERFORMANCE TASK ASSESSMENT LIST
DEER DILEMMA PERSUASIVE LETTER

Elements	Points Possible	Assessment Points Earned Assessment	
		Self	Teacher
1. The first paragraph clearly presents your opinion.	10	_____	_____
2. Based on our study of the science of population dynamics, at least five reasons are given for the increase in the deer population.	15	_____	_____
3. Each reason is explained.	15	_____	_____
4. At least two ideas are given to solve the problem.	10	_____	_____
5. Each idea for the solution is explained.	10	_____	_____
6. Ideas are presented in a logical order.	10	_____	_____
7. Technical vocabulary is used correctly.	5	_____	_____
8. Vocabulary is used to appeal to the audience.	10	_____	_____
9. The writing stays on the topic throughout.	5	_____	_____
10. A strong ending sums up the position.	10	_____	_____
TOTAL:	100	_____	_____

FIRST DRAFT OF LETTER

The problem of overpopulation of deer in Putnam Park is getting out of hand. Some people want many deer to be eliminated and others do not want the deer to be murdered. First I will explain how the deer population got so big, then I will explain the consequences of that overpopulation, and finally I will explain why I think that the deer herd must be reduced in size both by limited hunting and by sterilization of many of the females.

Over the last years the deer herd has gained access to more food and been protected from its predators. As the forests have been partially cleared to make room for recreational areas in the park more food is available to the deer. Also, when homes are built in the areas adjoining the park more food is available to them. At the same time that the carrying capacity of Putnam Park and its surrounding areas has increased the predators have been eliminated. No wonder that the population of deer has gotten bigger.

In addition to the more abundant food and the reduced predation, some people are feeding the deer in the winter. Usually some deer would die when food is in short supply. So, in reality, these well-meaning people are supporting a deer herd that is too large for the natural environment.

This overpopulation of deer is causing health and safety problems for people. First, according to the State Department of Public Health, Lyme Disease is a health problem in our State. Since 1993, there has been an increase in Lyme Disease in Putnam County. The tiny deer tick is the carrier of this disease.

Another health and safety problem is the automobile accidents caused by deer running across the roads in the areas around Putnam Park. As the deer go back and forth across the roads to visit their food supplies, they run into cars. According to the State Highway Patrol, some traffic accidents are caused by deer on the roads around Putnam Park. Several of these accidents have causes injuries and people were taken to the hospital. If there were less deer, the roads would be safer. The deer population in Putnam Park must be reduced now.

I am in support of a plan to thin the deer herd by killing some of the Putnam Park deer immediately and then using drugs to sterilize many of the females. I also recommend that the people who live around Putnam Park be educated to not feed the deer in the winter.

Please take my advice.

Sincerely,
Peter J.

PERFORMANCE TASK ASSESSMENT LIST
DEER DILEMMA PERSUASIVE LETTER

Elements	Points Possible	Assessment Points — Earned Assessment		
		Self	Peers	Teacher
1. The first paragraph clearly presents your opinion.	10	___	10	___
2. Based on our study of the science of population dynamics, at least five reasons are given for the increase in the deer population.	15	___	15	___
3. Each reason is explained.	15	___	8	___
4. At least two ideas are given to solve the problem.	10	___	10	___
5. Each idea for the solution is explained.	10	___	5	___
6. Ideas are presented in a logical order.	10	___	8	___
7. Technical vocabulary is used correctly.	5	___	2	___
8. Vocabulary is used to appeal to the audience.	10	___	4	___
9. The writing stays on the topic throughout.	5	___	5	___
10. A strong ending sums up the position.	10	___	5	___
TOTAL:	100	___	72	___

SECOND DRAFT OF LETTER

Dear Madam Commissioner,

The problem of overpopulation of deer in Putnam Park is getting out of hand and I applaud your concern over this issue. Some people are demanding that many deer be eliminated and others are pleading that you to have compassion for the deer. This is a tough decision for you to make. First I will explain how the deer population got so big, then I will explain the consequences of that overpopulation, and finally I will explain why I think that the deer herd must be reduced in size both by limited hunting and by sterilization of many of the does. In the long run, reducing the size of the deer herd is the kindest thing you can do for the deer.

Over the last years the deer herd has gained access to more food and been protected from its predators. As the forests have been partially cleared to make room for recreational areas in the park, the grassy play areas and the woody shrubs around the edges of all those open spaces have provided much more food for the deer than the sparse undergrowth a mature forest would have provided. Also, when homes are built in the areas adjoining the park, the lawns and ornamental plantings provide additional food for the deer. At the same time that the carrying capacity of Putnam Park and its surrounding areas has increased, wolves, coyotes, and domestic dogs have all been eliminated as deer hunters. The other predator, the human hunter, has also been banned. Sick, older, and less able deer are less likely to be culled from the herd. No wonder that the population of deer has skyrocketed.

In addition to the more abundant food sources and the reduced predation, the newspapers reported that some local residents have formed a club to feed the deer during the winter. They think that they are doing the deer a favor of making it easier for them to find food. Usually some deer would die when food is in short supply. So, in reality, these well-meaning people are supporting a deer herd that is too large for the natural environment. Man has caused the problem by disturbing the balance of nature.

This overpopulation of deer is causing health and safety problems for people. First, according to the State Department of Public Health, Lyme Disease is a health problem in our State. Since 1993, there has been a 23 percent increase in Lyme Disease in Putnam County. The tiny deer tick is the carrier of this disease and children and their parents who play games, take hikes, and have picnics in Putnam Park are in danger there. How many more people will get sick from Lyme Disease before action is taken?

Another serious health and safety problem is the automobile accidents caused by deer running across the roads in the areas around Putnam Park. As the deer go back and forth across the roads to visit their food supplies, they run into cars. According to the State Highway Patrol, there have been seven traffic accidents caused by deer so far this year on the roads around Putnam Park. Several of these accidents have causes serious injuries and people were taken to the hospital. It is a terrible thing to see a dead deer by the side of the road. It is worse to see a smashed car with injured children in it. These kinds of accidents can happen when a car hits a deer or when the car hits a tree after trying to avoid the deer suddenly jumping out onto the road. If there were less deer, the roads would be safer. The deer population in Putnam Park must be reduced now.

I am in support of a plan to thin the deer herd by killing some of the Putnam Park deer immediately and then using drugs to sterilize many of the does so that the population will remain low and hunting will not be necessary in the future. I also recommend that the people who live around Putnam Park be educated to not feed the deer in the winter. To make the hunt provide some good for people, I suggest that the deer meat could be ground up into deerburger and given away to needy people. My grandfather said that making deerburgers out of deer meat was the best way to use the whole deer so none would go to waste. Good meat would be great for these hungry people. I know that killing the deer would be a sad thing, but the meat would help parents feed their children.

This is a hard decision for you. My vote is for the safety of people and for the balance to nature to be restored. I respectfully urge you to support my plan.

Sincerely,

Peter J.

PERFORMANCE TASK ASSESSMENT LIST
DEER DILEMMA PERSUASIVE LETTER

Elements	Points Possible	Assessment Points Earned Assessment		
		Self	Peers	Teacher
1. The first paragraph clearly presents your opinion.	10	10	10	10
2. Based on our study of the science of population dynamics, at least five reasons are given for the increase in the deer population.	15	15	15	15
3. Each reason is explained.	15	10	12	12
4. At least two ideas are given to solve the problem.	10	10	10	10
5. Each idea for the solution is explained.	10	10	8	7
6. Ideas are presented in a logical order.	10	10	10	10
7. Technical vocabulary is used correctly.	5	10	2	10
8. Vocabulary is used to appeal to the audience.	10	5	4	4
9. The writing stays on the topic throughout.	5	5	5	4
10. A strong ending sums up the position.	10	8	6	8
TOTAL:	100	91	72	90

Electric Circuits
Performance Task

Background

A science textbook writer is looking for some new diagrams of series and parallel electric circuits. She has asked you to submit a drawing of each type of circuit with arrows showing the path of electricity in each circuit.

Task

Your job is to draw two circuits. One is a series circuit and the other is a parallel circuit. Each circuit has one battery, wire, a switch, and two light bulbs.

To prove that your drawings are correct, use the materials in your science kit to make each circuit the way you have drawn it.

When you complete drawing and making the two circuits, you will answer these two questions:

- What is the one important difference between a series and a parallel circuit?
- Why do you think that difference is the most important difference?

Audience

The audience for your drawing is elementary school children just beginning to learn about electricity.

Purpose

The purpose of your work is to use your knowledge of science to draw and make diagrams of electric circuits that are easy to understand.

Procedure

1. Use the assessment list for Electric Circuits.
2. Draw the series circuit. Use arrows to show the path of the electricity in the circuit.
3. Make the series circuit you have drawn.
4. Draw the parallel circuit. Use arrows to show the path of the electricity in the circuit.
5. Make the parallel circuit you have drawn.
6. Answer the two questions.

PERFORMANCE TASK ASSESSMENT LIST
ELECTRIC CIRCUITS

---

1. **Drawing of the series circuit using one battery, wire, switch, and two bulbs.**

   T: The circuit is drawn correctly so that it would work as a series circuit. The drawing is neat, organized, clear, and large.

   O: The circuit is drawn correctly so that it would work. The drawing is not clear or neat enough.

   W: The circuit is drawn so that it would not work as a series circuit.

2. **The constructed series circuit using one battery, wire, switch, and two bulbs.**

   T: The circuit is made so that is works as a series circuit. All work is neat and organized.

   O: The circuit is made so that it works but the work is not neat or organized enough.

   W: The circuit does not work as a series circuit.

3. **Drawing of the parallel circuit using one battery, wire, switch, and two bulbs.**

   T: The circuit is drawn correctly so that it would work as a parallel circuit. The drawing is neat, organized, clear, and large.

   O: The circuit is drawn correctly so that it would work. The drawing is not clear or neat enough.

   W: The circuit is drawn so that it would not work as a parallel circuit.

4. **The constructed parallel circuit using one battery, wire, switch, and two bulbs.**

   T: The circuit is made so that it works as a parallel circuit. All work is neat and organized.

   O: The circuit is made so that it works but the work is not neat or organized enough.

   W: The circuit does not work as a series circuit.

5. **The Venn Diagram**

  T: The Venn diagram shows at least six ways the series and parallel circuits are the same and three ways they differ.

  O: The Venn diagram shows at least four ways the series and parallel circuits are the same and two ways they differ.

  W: The Venn diagram shows at least two ways the series and parallel circuits are the same and one way they differ.

6. **Written explanation of the most important difference between the series and parallel circuits.**

  T: The reason given clearly shows how the circuit wiring differs between the series and parallel circuit. The reasons include a description of the differences in the path of the electricity in the two different types of circuits.

  O: The reason given clearly shows how the circuit wiring differs between the series and parallel circuit. The explanation about the differences in the path of the electricity is not made, incomplete, or inaccurate.

Did I Do My Best Work?

Terrific   OK   Needs Work

SERIES CIRCUIT

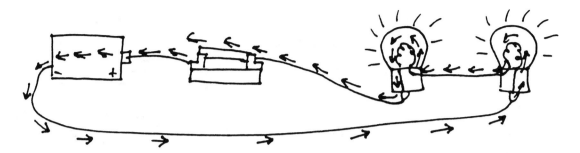

PARALLEL CIRCUIT

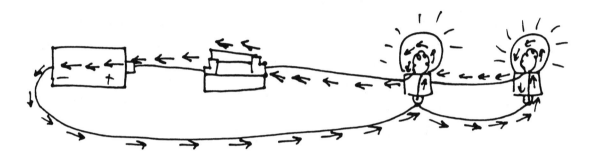

KEY

 Battery

— Wire

 Closed Switch

 Light Bulb with Light

→ Direction that the Electricity Moves

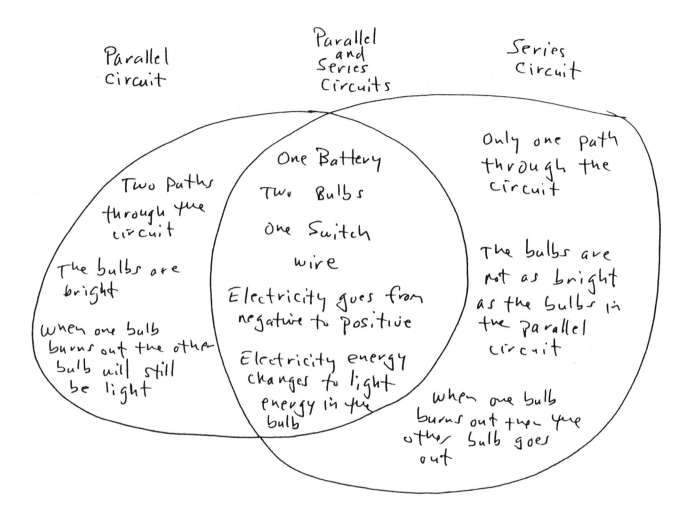

The most important difference between the series and the parallel circuits is how the electricity moves through the whole circuit. The electricity goes from the negative end of the battery through the wires and the small wires in the light bulbs back to the positive end of the battery in both the series and the parallel circuits. If the switch is open, the electricity does not move! In the series circuit, the electricity has only one path and that includes the little wire in the bulb. If that little wire burns out, then the electricity does not move, and that is like the switch is open. But in the parallel circuit, there is one path through the first light bulb and there is another path through the second light bulb. If the little wire in the first light bulb burns up, the electricity can still go through the second light bulb because the path to the second light bulb is not broken.

ELECTRIC ENERGY TRANSFORMATION AND TRANSFER PERFORMANCE TASK

Background

Look around you in our classroom. Where is electric energy being transferred and where is electric energy being transformed? The overhead projector is a machine that we use almost every day in our classroom. How is energy transfer and transformation important to how the overhead projector works?

This task you will do today is the beginning of a project to investigate and label many machines and pieces of equipment in our school to show where electric energy is being transferred and transformed.

Task

Your task is to use what you have learned about energy transfer and transformation from our work with batteries, wires, bulbs, and other devices to explain how energy transfer and transformation is happening in the overhead projector.

For this task, the "system" we will study starts with the electric power lines that come to our school and ends with the overhead projector.

Your work will be in the form of a diagram and a written explanation.

Audience

The audience for your work with the overhead projector is me, your teacher. The audience for the work you will do in labeling machines and equipment is your parents and other family members who will be coming to Open House next week.

Purpose

The purpose of your work is to help people gain a deeper understanding of how important energy transfer and transformation is in our lives.

Procedure

Safety: **You learned that the electric energy from the one battery can hurt you if you are not careful. The electric energy from the wall socket is much more dangerous. When you make observations of**

equipment and machines to study changes in electric energy, do not touch anything.

1. When you inspect the overhead projector, you may not touch it.

2. Review the assessment tool that will be used to assess your work.

3. Make a sketch of the "overhead projector system" and label where electric energy is being transferred and where it is being transformed.

4. Write your explanation.

5. Check your work with the assessment tool.

6. Revise as necessary.

7. You have 30 minutes to complete this task.

8. You will submit your labeled diagram of the overhead projector system and your written explanation.

PERFORMANCE TASK ASSESSMENT LIST
ELECTRIC ENERGY TRANSFORMATION AND TRANSFER

Elements	Points Possible	Assessment Points Earned Assessment	
		Self	Teacher
1. The explanation of energy transfer is accurate.	15	_____	_____
2. The explanation of energy transformation is accurate.	20	_____	_____
3. The science vocabulary about energy is used correctly.	10	_____	_____
4. The diagram is clear, organized, and helps support the written explanation.	20	_____	_____
5. Each paragraph has a clear main idea.	5	_____	_____
6. There are three supporting details for each main idea.	15	_____	_____
7. Signal words are used to indicate the sequence of the information in the whole piece.	9	_____	_____
8. There is agreement between nouns and verbs.	3	_____	_____
9. The handwriting is legible.	3	_____	_____
TOTAL:	100	_____	_____

STUDENT RESPONSE TO ELECTRIC
ENERGY TRANSFORMATION AND TRANSFER

Linda P.

Electric energy takes a path from the wires coming to our school, then through the wires in the walls, next into the cord for the overhead projector, after that the electric energy goes through some of the parts of the overhead projector, and finally it goes back through the wires. During this trip electric energy is transferred and transformed.

Electric energy is transferred from conductor to conductor. First the wire leading to our school is a conductor. The wires in the walls of the school are conductors. The wires in the cords for the overhead projector are conductors. The metal parts of the fan motor and the light bulb are conductors too. The electric energy stays electric energy in all these conductors. My pictures shows all these things.

The light bulb and the fan motor are like the stuff we used in the science project when we made parallel and series circuits. The electric energy is transformed to light energy in the light bulb. The light from the light bulb goes up to hit the little mirror on the arm of the overhead projector and then goes to the screen to show us what is on the overhead projector. The electric energy is transformed to movement energy in the fan motor. The fan motor turns the fan. I think that electric energy is also changed into sound energy because I can hear the fan motor running. I could also feel the hot air from the fan so some of the electric energy is changed to heat energy like in the motor I used for my circuit project because when I felt my little motor, I could feel it getting hot if it ran for a long time. There is a little sign on the overhead projector that says do not touch the light bulb because it gets hot so that must mean that some of the light energy changes to heat energy and that is where some of the heat comes from I feel in the hot air blowing out by the fan.

I think that the light bulb and the fan are in a parallel circuit like my picture shows because the motor can be on when the light is turned off. And I think that the switch on the overhead projector is for the light bulb only because I can turn the light bulb off and the motor still runs. Maybe there is a switch somewhere for the motor because it is not on all the time when the overhead projector is plugged into the wall socket.

(Student response continues on next page.)

STUDENT RESPONSE, CONTINUED

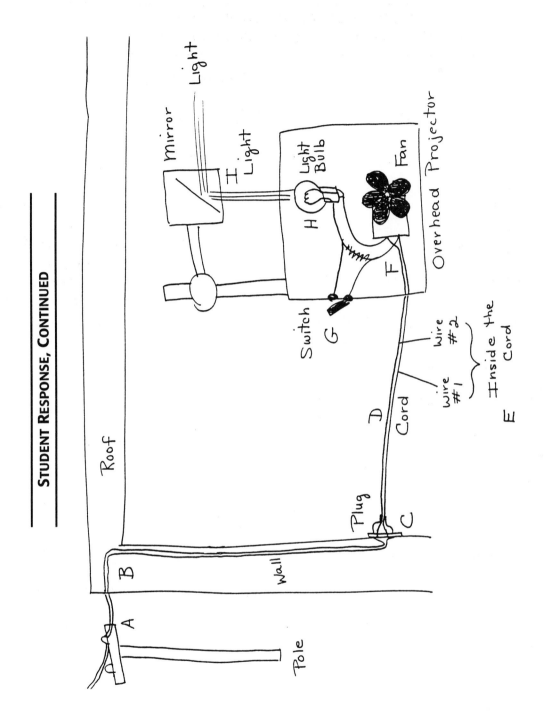

PERFORMANCE TASK ASSESSMENT LIST
ELECTRIC ENERGY TRANSFORMATION AND TRANSFER

Elements	Points Possible	Earned Assessment	
		Self	*Teacher*
1. The explanation of energy transfer is accurate.	15	15	15
2. The explanation of energy transformation is accurate.	20	19	15
3. The science vocabulary about energy is used correctly.	10	10	8
4. The diagram is clear, organized, and helps support the written explanation.	20	18	20
5. Each paragraph has a clear main idea.	5	5	5
6. There are three supporting details for each main idea.	15	15	15
7. Signal words are used to indicate the sequence of the information in the whole piece.	9	7	5
8. There is agreement between nouns and verbs.	3	3	3
9. The handwriting is legible.	3	3	3
TOTAL:	100	95	89

What about electric energy to sound? Light to heat?

B+

FORENSIC SCIENTIST
PERFORMANCE TASK

Background

A forensic scientist is a doctor who collects and examines data from bodies and crime scenes to learn about the causes of death. A forensic scientist can learn a lot about a person from just a few bones. For example, a forensic scientist can tell how tall a person was by measuring the length of a certain long bone.

Task

Your job is to determine which of the 10 long bones in the human body is the best predictor of the total height of a middle school student. For this task you will select one of the long bones of the arm and one of the long bones of the leg and determine which of these two long bones is the best predictor of the height of a middle school student.

Audience

The audience for your research is the forensic scientists who will read the report you will write for the *American Journal of Forensic Medicine*.

Purpose

The purpose of your work is to tell forensic scientists which long bone is the best predictor of a middle school student's total height.

Procedure

1. Read the assessment list for the Forensic Scientist task.

2. Select one arm long bone and one leg long bone to use for your study.

3. Collect data.

4. Organize your data into a data table.

5. Make a line graph of your data.

6. Write a summary of your graph.

Note: The data chart, the graph, and the written summary will be the article for the *American Journal of Forensic Medicine*.

PERFORMANCE TASK ASSESSMENT LIST
FORENSIC SCIENTIST

Elements	Points Possible	Assessment Points Earned Assessment Self	Teacher
1. The student restated the problem in his or her own words.	____	____	____
2. A plan for collecting data includes a statistically sound explanation of which middle school students to measure.	____	____	____
3. A plan for collecting data includes a statistically sound explanation of how many middle school students to measure.	____	____	____
4. Measurements are made using the metric system.	____	____	____
5. Data are organized into a well-labeled data table.	____	____	____
6. The data are displayed on a line graph.	____	____	____
7. The written summary states the conclusion.	____	____	____
8. The conclusion is supported by referring to specific data from the graph.	____	____	____
9. Technical vocabulary is used in the written summary.	____	____	____
10. The work is neat and organized.	____	____	____
TOTAL:	____	____	____

HEARTBEAT
PERFORMANCE TASK

Background

Exercise is important for good health. Aerobic exercise helps keep your heart and lungs in good shape. If you had only one minute to do a safe aerobic exercise, which aerobic exercise is best?

Task

Your job is to collect some data on how aerobic exercises influence your body's cardiovascular system. You will measure the influences that doing one minute of two different aerobic exercises has on the rate of your heat beat and use a bar graph to display the data.

Note: You must get approval from your Physical Education teacher to do the aerobic exercises you selected.

Audience

Your research will be posted in the gym in our town where people go for exercise.

Purpose

The purpose of your work is to inform the people who visit the gym about how different aerobic exercises influence the rate of heartbeat.

Procedure

1. Read the assessment list for the Heartbeat task.

2. Select two aerobic exercises to test.

3. Get permission from your Physical Education Teacher to do those two aerobic exercises.

4. Collect data.

5. Organize your data into a data table.

6. Make a bar graph of your data.

7. Write a summary of your graph.

Note: The graph and the written summary will be posted in the town's gym.

PERFORMANCE TASK ASSESSMENT LIST
HEARTBEAT

Elements	Points Possible	Earned Assessment Self	Teacher
1. The student restated the problem in his or her own words.	____	____	____
2. The student identified which data are about the independent variable and which data are about the dependent variable.	____	____	____
3. The data table that the student designed for the data included:	____	____	____
a. A way to show data from two aerobic exercises.	____	____	____
b. A way to show data from multiple trials.	____	____	____
c. A way to show actual data and averages.	____	____	____
4. The data table was well labeled and had an appropriate title.	____	____	____
5. The bar graph that the student designed for the data included:	____	____	____
a. A way to show the averages from each of the two types of aerobic exercises.			
b. The independent variable was plotted on the X axis and the dependent variable was plotted on the Y axis.			
6. The scales used on each axis allowed the whole space of the graph to be used efficiently.	____	____	____
7. The graph was well labeled and had a good title.	____	____	____
8. Color, texture, or some other graphic strategy is used to make the information on the graph clear.	____	____	____
9. A key clearly explains the symbols on the graph.	____	____	____
10. The written summary briefly and clearly summarizes the experiment.	____	____	____
11. The written summary states the conclusion.	____	____	____
12. Specific data from the graph are used to support the conclusion.	____	____	____
TOTAL:	____	____	____

INSECT MOUTH PARTS
PERFORMANCE TASK

Background

OUCH! Did an insect ever bite you? All of those bites hurt, but the way insects bite you depends on the type of mouth that the insect has.

Some insects are pests, but many insects are beneficial. Examples of beneficial insects are bees that pollinate crops and ladybugs that eat aphids that are harmful to crops.

Task

Your task is to make a detailed scientific drawing of the heads of two insects. Draw the head of an insect that is a pest and the head of an insect that is helpful.

Audience

We are making a gallery of "Pests and Helpers" and your drawings will be added to the collection.

Purpose

The purpose of your drawing is to show how the mouth parts of insects work to do their jobs.

Procedure

1. Review the assessment list for this task.

2. Select the two insect heads to draw. Get approval from your teacher for the heads you selected to draw.

3. Use the microscope to examine the heads as you make your drawings.

PERFORMANCE TASK ASSESSMENT LIST
INSECT MOUTH PARTS

Elements	Points Possible	Assessment Points Earned Assessment	
		Self	Teacher
1. A preliminary sketch shows how the final drawing will be laid out.	____	____	____
2. The mouth parts are clearly shown as the focus of the drawings.	____	____	____
3. At least two perspectives are drawn.	____	____	____
4. The drawings are done to scale.	____	____	____
5. The mouth parts are shown in detail.	____	____	____
6. Accurate labels and short annotations are used to explain how the mouth parts get food for the insect.	____	____	____
7. Color, texture, and other graphics are used to make the drawings easy to understand.	____	____	____
8. The work is extremely neat.	____	____	____
TOTAL:	____	____	____

INVENT A MUSICAL INSTRUMENT
PERFORMANCE TASK

Background

Making music is an important characteristic of humans. People have invented musical instruments for as long as there have been humans in existence.

Task

Your task is to invent a musical instrument that meets the design criteria listed at the end of this task.

Audience

Students who invent musical instruments that really work will form a band and learn to play one piece of music for a school assembly.

Purpose

The purpose of this performance task is for you to use the science of sound and your own creativity to make a musical instrument.

Procedure

1. Study the assessment list for Invent a Musical Instrument.
2. Study the design criteria.
3. Make a plan for your instrument.
4. Make the instrument.
5. Test your instrument to be sure it meets the design criteria.
6. Improve your instrument.
7. Turn in the following:
    A. A plan for your instrument.
    B. Your instrument.
    C. A written explanation supported by sketches that explains how your instrument makes sound at different pitches.

Design Criteria

1. No larger than 36 inches by 18 inches by 12 inches.
2. Made entirely of recycled materials.
3. Sturdy and safe.
4. Produces sound acoustically rather than electronically.
5. Can produce the 8-note diatonic scale or the 7-note Blues scale.
6. Can be tuned.
7. Can be used to vary rhythm and dynamics of the music played on this instrument.
8. Can be heard by anyone in the classroom without amplification.

PERFORMANCE TASK ASSESSMENT LIST
INVENT A MUSICAL INSTRUMENT

Elements	Points Possible	Assessment Points Earned Assessment		
		Self	Peers	Teacher
1. The plan shows the structure of the instrument from at least two perspectives.	_____	_____	_____	_____
2. Labels and annotations on the plan show how the sound will be produced.	_____	_____	_____	_____
3. Labels and annotations on the plan will show how recycled materials will be used.	_____	_____	_____	_____
4. The instrument meets all design criteria.	_____	_____	_____	_____
a. Meets size criteria.	_____	_____	_____	_____
b. Is made entirely of recycled materials.	_____	_____	_____	_____
c. Produces sound acoustically.	_____	_____	_____	_____
d. Produces the 8-note diatonic scale or the 7-note Blues scale.	_____	_____	_____	_____
e. Can be tuned.	_____	_____	_____	_____
f. Is used to vary dynamics of the sound.	_____	_____	_____	_____
g. Is used to vary rhythm of the sound.	_____	_____	_____	_____
h. Is sturdy and safe.	_____	_____	_____	_____
I. Can be heard by everyone in the classroom without electronic amplification.	_____	_____	_____	_____
5. The work on the instrument shows care and craftsmanship.	_____	_____	_____	_____
6. The written explanation describes how the instrument makes acoustic sound.	_____	_____	_____	_____
7. The written explanation describes how the instrument makes acoustic sound at each of the notes of its scale.	_____	_____	_____	_____
8. Detailed sketches support the writing to show the science behind how the instrument works.	_____	_____	_____	_____
9. The writing is organized and it is easy to follow the explanation.	_____	_____	_____	_____
TOTAL:	_____	_____	_____	_____

INVENT A WORM FARM FOR MAKING SOIL
PERFORMANCE TASK

Background

Think about the little scraps of raw vegetables thrown away at your house every day. Wouldn't it be good to recycle those old vegetables into new soil? Worms play an important part in turning old vegetation into new soil. How can worms be used in the home to recycle these raw vegetables?

Task

Your task is to invent a worm farm for the home or apartment that can recycle old, raw vegetables into new soil. Your invention must meet the design criteria listed at the end of this page.

Audience

Inventions that work will be submitted as ideas to the Student Council, which is looking for fundraisers. Your invention may be mass-produced and sold to help raise money to support the Spring Field Day in May.

Purpose

The purpose of this performance task is for you to use what you know about the life needs of worms to invent a worm farm that people would not mind having in their homes or apartments.

Procedure

1. Study the assessment list for Invent a Worm Farm.

2. Study the design criteria.

3. Make a plan for your worm farm.

4. Make the worm farm.

5. Test your worm farm for one month in your home or apartment to be sure it meets the design criteria.

6. Improve your worm farm.

7. Turn in the following:

    A. A plan for your worm farm.

    B. Your worm farm

C. A written explanation supported by sketches that explains how your worm farm meets the life needs of the worms.

D. A letter from your parents that verifies that you did all the work on the worm farm yourself and that the worm farm was used in your own home or apartment for one month.

Design Criteria

1. No larger than 24 inches by 18 inches by 12 inches.

2. Made of recycled materials entirely.

3. Sturdy and safe.

4. Keeps at least 250 red wigglers or 100 earth worms alive and healthy.

5. Can process at least one cup of raw, finely chopped vegetables a day.

6. Turns the raw vegetables into soil within one month.

7. Does not produce any bad odors.

8. Is decorated creatively.

PERFORMANCE TASK ASSESSMENT LIST
INVENT A WORM FARM

(See the place for parents to assess the worm farm.)

Elements	Points Possible	Assessment Points Earned Assessment		
		Self	Parent	Teacher
1. The plan shows the structure of the worm farm from at least two perspectives.	_____	_____	_____	_____
2. Labels and annotations on the plan show how the worm farm will meet the life needs of worms.	_____	_____	_____	_____
3. Labels and annotations on the plan will show how recycled materials will be used.	_____	_____	_____	_____
4. The worm farm meets all design criteria.	_____	_____	_____	_____
5. The work on the worm farm shows care and craftsmanship.	_____	_____	_____	_____
6. The written explanation describes how the worm farm meets the life needs of worms.	_____	_____	_____	_____
7. The written explanation describes how the worm farm turns raw vegetables into new soil.	_____	_____	_____	_____
8. Sketches support the writing to show the science behind how the worm farm works.	_____	_____	_____	_____
9. Each paragraph has a clear main idea.	_____	_____	_____	_____
10. There are enough details to support each main idea.	_____	_____	_____	_____
11. The writing is organized and it is easy to follow the explanation.	_____	_____	_____	_____
12. The letter that verifies that you did all the work on the worm farm yourself and that the worm farm was used successfully in your home or apartment for one month.	_____	_____	_____	_____
TOTAL:	_____	_____	_____	_____

MACHINE SKIT
PERFORMANCE TASK

Background

A machine is a complex tool that has several working parts. Each part has a job to do in the overall working of the machine. When all the parts work together properly, the whole machine works properly.

Task

Your task is to work with three other students to invent a machine that has four working and interrelated parts. Each member of your group will be one of those working parts. The four of you will "become the machine."

Audience

Your presentations will be videotaped and the excellent ones will be shown at the Museum for Technology and Science.

Purpose

The purpose of your skit is to teach and entertain the people who visit the museum.

Procedure

1. Review the assessment list for a Machine Skit.
2. Select the overall job that your four-part machine will do. Give your machine a name and make a written explanation of the overall job of your machine.
3. Design how each of the four parts of the machine will work.
4. Design how each of the four parts fits together to make the whole machine accomplish its overall purpose.
5. Complete a planning form for your machine skit.
6. Complete a drawn plan for your four-part machine.
7. Write an explanation of the structure and function of each part of the machine and how that part fits into the overall workings of the machine.
8. Decide which person in your group will be which of part of the machine.
9. Plan for any props and/or costumes that will be needed.
10. Practice your machine skit. Your skit must be between 45 and 60 seconds.
11. Revise your machine skit and present it to our class.

PERFORMANCE TASK ASSESSMENT LIST
MACHINE SKIT

Elements	Points Possible	*Assessment Points* Earned Assessment		
		Self	Peers	Teacher
1. The plan explains the detailed function of each part through sketches and written explanation.	_____	_____	_____	_____
2. The plan shows how all four parts of the machine work together.	_____	_____	_____	_____
3. By the time the skit is over it is clear what the overall function of the machine is.	_____	_____	_____	_____
4. Each part of the machine has a specific and different function as shown through the action of the student pretending to be that part.	_____	_____	_____	_____
5. The function of each part is dramatic and easy to see.	_____	_____	_____	_____
6. Each part has a particular sound effect that goes with its action.	_____	_____	_____	_____
7. All four parts fit together in some planned way.	_____	_____	_____	_____
8. The action of one part directly influences the action of another part.	_____	_____	_____	_____
9. The skit lasts between 45 and 60 seconds.	_____	_____	_____	_____
TOTAL:	_____	_____	_____	_____

MODEL OF HOW AN ENZYME WORKS
PERFORMANCE TASK

Background

When we mixed ground-up raw potatoes with 3% hydrogen peroxide solution, a vigorous reaction occurred with the obvious production of gas. Upon testing, that gas was discovered to be oxygen. When ground-up cooked potato was mixed with 3% hydrogen peroxide solution, nothing happened. Our science book tells us that an enzyme called hydrogen peroxidase is in most living cells. Hydrogen peroxidase catalyzes the breakdown of hydrogen peroxide into water and oxygen gas. This is good because if the hydrogen peroxide was not destroyed, it would destroy the cell. Enzymes are proteins that can easily be destroyed by heat.

Task

Your task is to make a three-dimensional model of hydrogen peroxide and the enzyme hydrogen peroxidase to help show the science behind how an enzyme works.

Audience

The audience for this model is the students who take this course next year.

Purpose

The purpose of your model is to show the science behind how an enzyme works.

Procedure

1. Study the assessment list for the Model of Enzyme Action.
2. Make a sketch of the three-dimensional models you will build. Show at least two perspectives.
3. Label and annotate your sketch to show:
   A. The science principles in how a enzyme works.
   B. The materials you will use to build the models.
4. Make a list of how the model is an INACCURATE representation of how an enzyme works.
5. Make the three-dimensional model.
6. Complete a written explanation of the how the model shows what happens when hydrogen peroxide and hydrogen peroxidase mix.

PERFORMANCE TASK ASSESSMENT LIST
MODEL OF HOW AN ENZYME WORKS

Elements	Points Possible	Self	Peers	Teacher
		Assessment Points		
		Earned Assessment		
1. The plan shows the three-dimensional model from at least two perspectives.	____	____	____	____
2. The plan shows an accurate use of the "Lock and Key" principle of the action of enzymes.	____	____	____	____
3. The plan shows how the sequence of events in the reaction between hydrogen peroxide and hydrogen peroxidase.	____	____	____	____
4. The plan is annotated to accurately show the science behind how enzymes work.	____	____	____	____
5. The plan is annotated to show what materials will be used to make the models.	____	____	____	____
6. Color, texture, and other graphic devices are used to make the plan easier to understand.	____	____	____	____
7. A list is made of at least six ways the model is really an INACCURATE representation of the real reaction.	____	____	____	____
8. The three-dimensional model can be used to show what happens when hydrogen peroxide and hydrogen peroxidase mix.	____	____	____	____
9. The three-dimensional model is durable.	____	____	____	____
10. The written explanation describes how the model is to be used to show the steps in the reaction between hydrogen peroxide and hydrogen peroxidase.	____	____	____	____
11. The written explanation is so complete that someone else could use the model to demonstrate the reaction.	____	____	____	____
12. The written explanation is scientifically accurate.	____	____	____	____
TOTAL:	____	____	____	____

ROLLING DOWN THE RIVER
PERFORMANCE TASK

Background

The Pine River Rafting and Canoe Club has given a grant to our class for us to help them on a project to make a model of the Pine River. The purpose of this model is to show where the rapids, the sandbars, current, and other features are on the Pine River. This model will help them plan trips and teach new rafters and canoeists how to be safe on the river.

Task

Each of you has been given a map that shows a part of the Pine River. Each of you has a different section of the river on your map. Your task is to show where the sandbars and the current are strongest on your part of the river.

After each person has completed their section of Pine River, we will put all the sections together to form one continuous model of a five-mile section of Pine River.

Audience

The audience for your map is the members of the Pine River Raft and Canoe Club.

Purpose

The purpose of your map and written explanation is to teach the members about the river.

Procedure

1. Review the assessment list for Rolling Down the River.

2. Study the section of the map you are given. Use this map as a graphic organizer to sketch where the current is and where the sandbar/sandbars is/are.

3. Make your final map.

4. Write an explanation of what the map shows.

5. Complete your self-assessment and ask a classmate to assess your work. Revise as necessary. You have one class period to make your map and write your explanation.

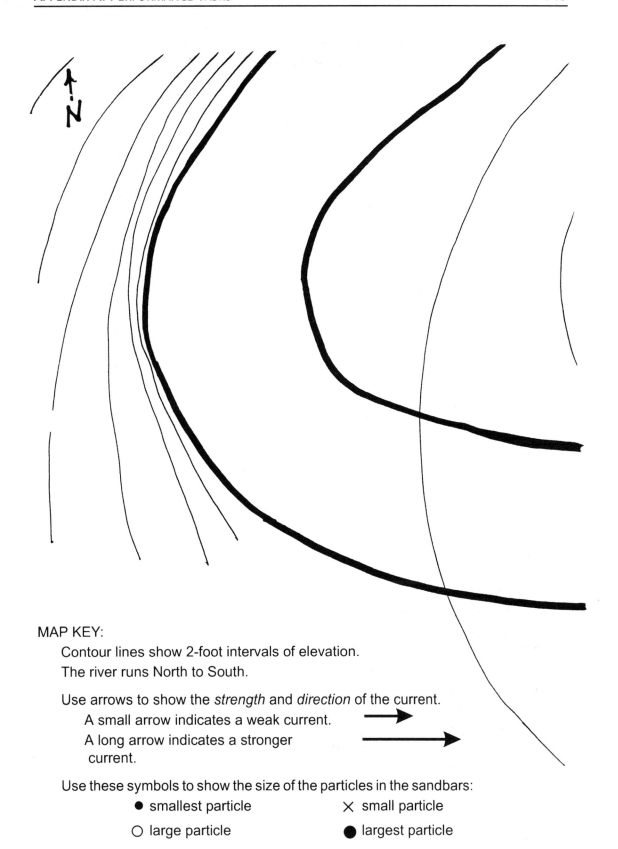

MAP KEY:

    Contour lines show 2-foot intervals of elevation.

    The river runs North to South.

    Use arrows to show the *strength* and *direction* of the current.

        A small arrow indicates a weak current.

        A long arrow indicates a stronger
      current.

    Use these symbols to show the size of the particles in the sandbars:

          ● smallest particle   ✕ small particle

          ○ large particle   ● largest particle

PERFORMANCE TASK ASSESSMENT LIST
ROLLING DOWN THE RIVER

Elements	Points Possible	Assessment Points Earned Assessment		
		Self	Peers	Teacher

Note: Points are given for providing correct and logically explained information.

THE MAP

1. Arrows show the direction of the current.	5	_____	_____	_____
2. Arrows show the strength of the current all along the river.	10	_____	_____	_____
3. At least one major sand bar is shown.	5	_____	_____	_____
4. The symbols for particle size are used to show the composition of the sand bar.	15	_____	_____	_____
5. Your work shows careful attention to details.	5	_____	_____	_____

THE WRITTEN EXPLANATION

6. Technical vocabulary is used correctly.	5	_____	_____	_____
7. The strength of the current is described and changes in the current strength along the river are explained.	10	_____	_____	_____
8. You give a clear explanation of why the sand bar you show is where it is.	10	_____	_____	_____
9. You give a clear explanation of why the particles are arranged the way you show them in your sand bar.	20	_____	_____	_____
10. Your writing is organized to show clear sequence.	5	_____	_____	_____
11. Your writing is organized to show clear cause and effect relationships	5	_____	_____	_____
12. Your writing stays on topic.	5	_____	_____	_____
TOTAL:	100	_____	_____	_____

NOTES TO THE TEACHER
ROLLING DOWN THE RIVER

During the Field Trip to the Stream or River

- Assure safety around water. Have water safety equipment handy.

- Have a minimum of one adult for every five students.

- Give students experience reading topographic maps to describe land forms around the stream or river.

- Give students hands-on experiences of seeing and feeling the composition of the sandbar from its upstream end to its downstream end.

- Give students experiences in sketching currents in relation to sandbar location and composition.

Work with the Stream Table

- Give students experience of making streambeds curving to the right and to the left and with various amounts of curve.

Vocabulary

- Keep a list of "river science" vocabulary and definitions on the chalkboard. Expect that vocabulary to be used in conversation and in writing.

Writing

- Model writing that shows excellent sequencing.

- Model how drawings and written explanations can be made to support each other.

Use of Real Gravel and Sand

- This task asks students to use symbols for sandbar material of different size. An engaging alternative is to give students actual gravel and sand (lima bean size, small pea size, large sand, fine sand each in its own container), glue, and cardboard, and ask them to make the sandbar where it would be on the river drawn on the cardboard.

Ashley R. (The student wrote this explanation with the help of a computer.)

The Pine River runs from north to south in its river bed that it has eroded out of the land. The material that is has eroded from the land is called its load. Certain parts of the current run fast and certain parts of the current slow down as the river winds its way through its river valley. The speeding up of the current is what causes erosion and the slowing down of the current is what causes sandbars to form through a process called deposition.

The riverbed runs from north to south because the land is higher at the top left part of the map than it is where the river ends at the mid-lower right-hand part of this map. Numerals 4 and 5 show a drop of four feet which means that the river is running down hill from where it begins on the map at numeral 1 to where it ends at numeral 6 on this map.

First the Pine River picks up its load of rocks, gravel, sand, and silt as its swift current eats into the banks that it hits. The current at point 2 is eroding the bank there and the load that it scoops up at point 2 is carried down stream to be deposited at locations not shown on this map.

Sandbars will form on the river where the current slows down and the water can not carry its load. The sandbar I drew on this map is made of rock, gravel, sand, and silt that the river gouged out of its banks upriver from point 1. As the current with its heavy load approaches the curve at point 6, some energy is lost from the current and the heaviest rocks drop out because the current does not have enough energy to carry them any further. As the current continues to slow down and lose energy the gravel drops out at about point 7 because the current no longer has the energy to carry it. The current slows down every further and the sand is dropped out at point 8. Finally, some fine clay slit falls out at point 9 where the current has the least energy. Very tiny particles may still be in the current as it moves down stream at point 10 because the current still has some energy. If all the energy was gone, the water would not move at all.

A better name for this bar would be a Rock-Gravel-Sand-Silt bar because the bar is made up of all those things not just sand. The shape of river and the location of its RGSS bars is caused by the energy in the water as the Pine River runs down hill.

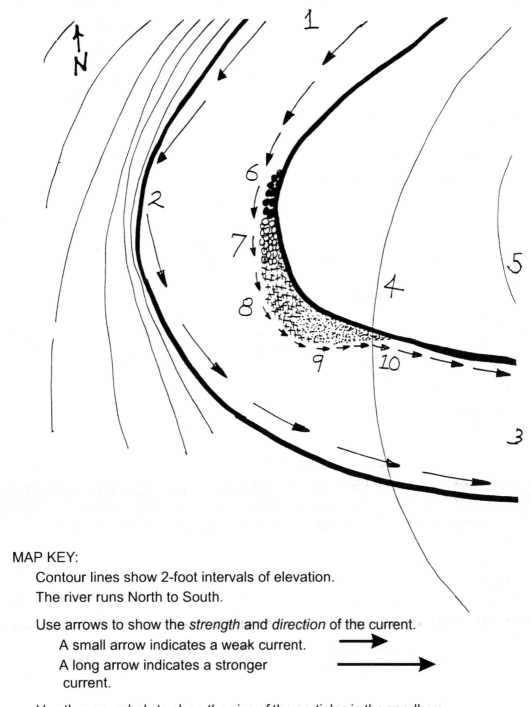

MAP KEY:

Contour lines show 2-foot intervals of elevation.
The river runs North to South.

Use arrows to show the *strength* and *direction* of the current.

A small arrow indicates a weak current.

A long arrow indicates a stronger
current.

Use these symbols to show the size of the particles in the sandbars:

● smallest particle   ✕ small particle

○ large particle   ● largest particle

PERFORMANCE TASK ASSESSMENT LIST
ROLLING DOWN THE RIVER

Elements	*Points Possible*	*Assessment Points Earned Assessment*		
		Self	*Peers*	*Teacher*
Note: Points are given for providing correct and logically explained information.				
THE MAP				
1. Arrows show the direction of the current.	5	5	5	5
2. Arrows show the strength of the current all along the river.	10	10	10	10
3. At least one major sand bar is shown.	5	5	5	5
4. The symbols for particle size are used to show the composition of the sand bar.	15	15	15	15
5. Your work shows careful attention to details.	5	5	5	5
THE WRITTEN EXPLANATION				
6. Technical vocabulary is used correctly.	5	4	5	5
7. The strength of the current is described and changes in the current strength along the river are explained.	10	10	6	8 What about the current in middle of the river?
8. You give a clear explanation of why the sand bar you show is where it is.	10	10	10	9
9. You give a clear explanation of why the particles are arranged the way you show them in your sand bar.	20	20	20	20
10. Your writing is organized to show clear sequence.	5	5	5	5
11. Your writing is organized to show clear cause and effect relationships	5	5	5	5
12. Your writing stays on topic.	5	5	5	5
TOTAL:	100	99	96	97

A+

STATES OF MATTER SKIT
PERFORMANCE TASK

Background

Some people learn science by reading about it. Some people learn science by doing experiments. And some people learn science by seeing other people act out a principle of science.

Task

Your task is to select one of the principles of science from this list and then plan and give a skit to explain the science behind that principle. *(You may suggest another principle of science to your teacher if you would like to do a skit about a principle of science that is not on this list.)*

- Principles of Science
  States of Matter   Photosynthesis
  The Chemistry of Rusting   How Light Travels Through a Prism
  Why a Red Shirt Looks Red   The Pitch of Sound
  Other with teacher approval

Audience

Your presentations will be videotaped and the excellent ones will be shown at the Open House next month.

Purpose

The purpose of your oral presentation is to teach science in an entertaining way.

Procedure

1. Review the assessment list for a skit.
2. Select the principle of science for your skit. No principle may be used by more than one student. Selection of principles of science will be on a first-come-first-serve basis.
3. Complete a planning form for your skit.
4. Complete a storyboard for your skit.
5. Plan for any characterizations that will be used in the skit.
6. Plan for any props and/or costumes that will be needed.
7. Annotate your storyboard to show who will say and do what.
8. Practice your skit. Your skit must be between 60 and 180 seconds.
9. Revise your skit and present it to our class.

PERFORMANCE TASK ASSESSMENT LIST
SCIENCE SKIT

Elements	Points Possible	Assessment Points Earned Assessment		
		Self	Peers	Teacher
1. The opening grabs the attention of the audience.	_____	_____	_____	_____
2. The science principle being shown is clear.	_____	_____	_____	_____
3. The sequence of events is correct and helps to explain the principle of science.	_____	_____	_____	_____
4. Visuals and/or props add to the skit and do not distract the audience.	_____	_____	_____	_____
5. Characterization through dialogue, costume, or some other strategy helps the audience understand the science principle being presented.	_____	_____	_____	_____
6. The skit is focused on the topic and does not get "off topic."	_____	_____	_____	_____
7. The skit has a memorable ending.	_____	_____	_____	_____
8. The speaker's voice is loud enough for all to hear if there is dialogue or vocal sound effects.	_____	_____	_____	_____
9. The skit lasts between 60 and 180 seconds.	_____	_____	_____	_____
TOTAL:	_____	_____	_____	_____

WHAT DO YOU EAT?
PERFORMANCE TASK

Background

Food is one of the most important parts of our lives. What do you eat?

Task

Your job is to collect some data on how many calories you get from each type of food you eat. You will categorize the food you eat in your largest meal of the day into these categories: Meat, Vegetables, Fruit, Grains/Cereals, Dairy, and Other.

You will put your data into a circle or pie graph.

Audience

Your research will be posted in the cafeteria of this school.

Purpose

The purpose of your work is to inform the students in our school about what students eat.

Procedure

1. Read the assessment list for the What Do You Eat? task.

2. Study the data table provided to you for this task.

3. Plan a strategy to collect data on what you eat and how much of each thing you eat during one day. Check this strategy with your teacher before you begin your study.

4. Use the calorie counter chart in class to determine the number of calories in specific quantities of each type of food you eat.

5. Collect data.

6. Organize your data into the data table.

7. Make a circle or pie graph of your data.

8. Write a summary of your circle or pie graph.

Note: The graph and the written summary will be posted in the cafeteria of this school.

PERFORMANCE TASK ASSESSMENT LIST
WHAT DO YOU EAT?

Elements	Points Possible	Earned Assessment Self	Teacher
BEFORE ANY DATA IS COLLECTED			
1. The student restated the problem in his or her own words.	_____	_____	_____
2. The student made a list of questions that he or she needed to answer for this study.	_____	_____	_____
3. The student stated a plan to answer each of these questions.	_____	_____	_____
DATA COLLECTION AND DISPLAY			
4. The student showed his or her computations to explain how the total number of calories for each food group was determined.	_____	_____	_____
5. The student showed his or her computations to explain how the percentages were calculated.	_____	_____	_____
6. Computations were accurate.	_____	_____	_____
7. All units were labeled.	_____	_____	_____
8. The data were accurately displayed on a circle or pie graph.	_____	_____	_____
9. The graph was well labeled and had an appropriate title.	_____	_____	_____
10. Color, texture, or some other graphic strategy was used to make the graph easy to understand.	_____	_____	_____
WRITTEN EXPLANATION			
11. The written summary clearly described what the graph showed.	_____	_____	_____
12. The data from the graph were described in a logical order in the written summary.	_____	_____	_____
13. Capitalization was used correctly.	_____	_____	_____
TOTAL:	_____	_____	_____

THE QUANTITY AND CALORIE CONTENT OF THE FOOD I
ATE IN MY LARGEST MEAL ON _____ (DAY)

FOOD GROUPS

	Meat	Vegetables	Fruit	Cereal/Grain	Dairy	Other	Total Calories
Quantity of Food							
Calorie Content of Food							
Percent of the Total Calories							

SCORING GUIDE FOR A SURVEY AND ITS ANALYSIS

From *A Collection of Performance Tasks and Rubrics: Middle School Mathematics* by Charlotte Danielson (Eye On Education, 1997).

	Level One	Level Two	Level Three	Level Four
Design of Survey Instrument	Questions very limited; will not serve to obtain necessary information.	Questions will elicit almost all information required for the task.	Questions will elicit all information required.	In addition, questions asked in a manner to ease later data analysis.
Analysis of Data	Data poorly organized; hard to read and interpret.	Data organization is uneven.	Data organized but difficult to use for making a graph.	Data well organized and neatly presented.
Quality of Graph	Graph seriously flawed; inappropriate type, inaccurate, or error in execution.	Graph has one serious error	Graph is appropriated to the data, and is accurate.	In addition, the graph is well presented, with all details well executed.
Mathematical Projections	Mathematical projections inaccurate, with no apparent method used.	Although inaccurate, projections show evidence of a method being used.	Mathematical projections essentially accurate.	In addition, the mathematical projections are imaginative in their methodology.
"Case" Made to Producer	Ideas are not accurately summarized, a producer could not act on the findings.	Minor errors in the interpretation of findings.	Interpretation of data essentially accurate; data support findings.	In addition, the findings are presented in an imaginative manner.

WORM PROJECT
PERFORMANCE TASK

Background

The third graders study earthworms and have a worm farm in their classroom. Each farm contains about 1,200 small worms called Red Wigglers and a few huge Night Crawlers. The third graders enjoy feeding the worms and watching them work the soil in the farm. The problem the third graders are having is that there is very little information about earthworms in their school library. And this is where you come in.

Task

Your task is to do some research on earthworms and create a information resource bank of written material, models, inventions, and/ or illustrations about earthworms.

Audience

The third grade students will use the information resources you make.

Purpose

The purpose of your work is to teach the third grades a lot about earthworms.

Procedure

1. Your task is divided into these components. Each piece has a description and an assessment list. Complete one component at a time and get it approved and assessed by the teacher.
    COMPONENT
    Selecting your research topic about worms.
    Finding and collecting information for your research topic.
    Organizing the information you find.
    Making your products that the third graders will use to learn about worms.

2. Before you go any further, discuss these questions with a partner:
    What is the goal of this whole project?
    What are third graders like and what kind of information resources will they like to use?
    How will the third graders assess the quality of the work we do for them?

WORM PROJECT:
SELECTING YOUR RESEARCH TOPIC

A. The third graders have six research questions about earthworms.

B. Brainstorm topics for each research question.

C. Use the assessment list for Selecting a Research Topic.

1. How many kinds of earthworms are there and what is each kind like?

2. What are the parts of an earthworm and how are those parts the same as and different from the parts of other animals?

3. What do earthworms need to stay alive and how do their parts help them live where they do?

4. What is the life cycle of an earthworm and how is that life cycle the same as and different from the life cycles of other animals?

5. How does the earthworm fit into the "balance of nature" and what would happen to that balance if earthworms became extinct?

6. Why do earthworms need people and why do people need earthworms?

****

D. From your list of possible research topics for each research question, select the three topics that are the most interesting to you.

E. Now from your list of three, select the one research topic that you can complete within this one-week project.

F. Write that research topic in the form of a question here.

G. What will you make for the third graders? List and describe your final product(s).

Type of Final Product   **Why This Product Will Be Good for the Third Graders**

PERFORMANCE TASK ASSESSMENT LIST
WORM PROJECT: SELECTING A RESEARCH TOPIC
AND FORMAT FOR A FINAL PRODUCT

Elements	Points Possible	Assessment Points Earned Assessment		
		Self	Peers	Teacher
1. I listed at least three research topics for each of the six research questions about worms.	24	_____	_____	_____
2. Each research idea is clearly stated as a complete sentence.	18	_____	_____	_____
3. I selected the three research topics that are most interesting to me.	9	_____	_____	_____
4. I made my final selection for a research topic that I can complete by the end of this three-week project.	5	_____	_____	_____
5. I stated my research topic in the form of a question that will direct my research.	4	_____	_____	_____
6. I described what I am planning to make for the third graders as the result of my research.	20	_____	_____	_____
7. I explained why my final product(s) will be useful and interesting to the third graders.	20	_____	_____	_____
TOTAL:	100	_____	_____	_____

WORM PROJECT:
FINDING AND COLLECTING INFORMATION
ON YOUR RESEARCH TOPIC

---

1. Restate your research question here:

2. List the sources of information that might be helpful to you. Books and reprints from magazine articles are on reserve in the library/Media Center. There are also several links to Web sites about worms on our school's science home page. You must use information from both print sources and from the web sites.

    Print

    Web Site Links

3. Circle the four information sources that you can actually use to give you good information. Explain why you selected each of those three.

The Four Best Sources   **Why the Source Will Probably Be a Good One**

Source #1

Source #2

Source #3

Source #4

4. Collect information using the note card system we have learned to use.

PERFORMANCE TASK ASSESSMENT LIST
WORM PROJECT: FINDING AND COLLECTING INFORMATION

Elements	Points Possible	Assessment Points Earned Assessment		
		Self	Peers	Teacher
SELECTING INFORMATION SOURCES				
1. I listed at least eight sources of information for my research topic.	16	_____	_____	_____
2. I included information sources in the categories of print, electronic, hands-on, and personal interview.	8	_____	_____	_____
3. I selected the four sources of information that I can use to get good quality information.	4	_____	_____	_____
4. I selected information from at least one print source and from at least one Web site source.	2	_____	_____	_____
5. I explained why I selected those four information sources.	10	_____	_____	_____
NOTE CARDS FOR COLLECTING INFORMATION				
6. Each note card has a title.	5	_____	_____	_____
7. Each note card has one item of information.	5	_____	_____	_____
8. Drawings are included as necessary.	5	_____	_____	_____
9. Information has been summarized rather than copied from the source.	20	_____	_____	_____
10. Full bibliographic information is included on each note card.	20	_____	_____	_____
11. Your name is on each note card.	5	_____	_____	_____
TOTAL:	100	_____	_____	_____

WORM PROJECT:
ORGANIZING INFORMATION COLLECTED

1. What kind of graphic organizer will be most helpful to you to organize the information from your note cards?

   Select one or more forms of a graphic organizer we have used.

2. Complete the graphic organizer.

3. Use the generic assessment list for the form of the graphic organizer you used.

WORM PROJECT:
MAKING THE FINAL PRODUCT(S)

1. Make a plan for making your final product.

2. Find a generic assessment list from our classroom collection of generic assessment lists that fits your final product.

3. Change that assessment list to be specifically about your worm project. Get your teacher's approval of the revised assessment list that you will use.

PERFORMANCE TASK ASSESSMENT LIST
WORM PROJECT: GROUP WORK

Elements	Points Possible	Assessment Points Earned Assessment		
		Self	Peers	Teacher
1. The individual comes to the group prepared to contribute.	_____	_____	_____	_____
2. The individual comes to the group having completed the homework or other assignments relevant to what the group will do.	_____	_____	_____	_____
3. The individual helps the group manage time.	_____	_____	_____	_____
4. The individual helps the group stay on task.	_____	_____	_____	_____
5. The individual helps the group follow the directions.	_____	_____	_____	_____
6. The individual encourages others to work and contribute.	_____	_____	_____	_____
7. The individual disagrees in a respectful manner.	_____	_____	_____	_____
8. The individual negotiates in a constructive manner.	_____	_____	_____	_____
9. The individual helps the group accurately assess its work together.	_____	_____	_____	_____
10. The individual helps the group set goals to improve the power of their collaboration.	_____	_____	_____	_____
TOTAL:	_____	_____	_____	_____

THE MANAGEMENT PLAN

Your Name: _____

Today's Date: _____   **Due Date for Final Product:** _____

Project Title: _____

****

List of Specific Tasks to Complete	Target Date for Completion	I Will Need Help on This Step From
Check Point # 1	_____	
Check Point #2	_____	
Final Product Handed In	_____	

****

Problems That Might Occur That Could Cause Me Trouble Keeping to This Plan	Strategies I Could Use to Overcome Those Problems and Stay on Schedule

_____   _____

Signed   **Date**

PERFORMANCE TASK ASSESSMENT LIST
MANAGEMENT PLAN

	Assessment Points		
Elements	*Points Possible*	*Earned Assessment*	
		Self	*Teacher*
1. I completed the information at the top of the form.	_____	_____	_____
2. I listed all the parts of my project in the order in which I must do them.	_____	_____	_____
3. Each item on my list is specific.	_____	_____	_____
4. I indicated the date I plan to complete each step.	_____	_____	_____
5. I included the check point items and due dates.	_____	_____	_____
6. I indicated who I could receive help from when I need it.	_____	_____	_____
7. I listed at least two things that might be considered problems that might keep me from staying on track and completing my work.	_____	_____	_____
8. For each problem I described, I also explained how I would overcome that problem.	_____	_____	_____
9. My management plan is neat and presentable.	_____	_____	_____
TOTAL:	_____	_____	_____

APPENDIX B

GRAPHIC ORGANIZERS

This appendix has samples of graphic organizers that are used as intermediate products or final products in performance tasks.

Each performance task has one or more thinking skill verbs that direct the processing of information for that performance task. These graphic organizers help the students do that processing. For example, if the performance task is to sequence the stage of the life cycle of the malaria parasite, then a "cycle sequence" graphic organizer is used. If the task is to compare and contrast the life cycles of a malaria parasite and a liver fluke, then a Venn diagram of some sort is used.

The performance task may ask only for a completed graphic organizer, or it may require that the graphic organizer be done as a "prewriting" step for a written explanation of some sort.

Remember that the ultimate goal of education is for students to be independent learners. Students should eventually be able to construct and use graphic organizers on their own with no prompting from the teacher. To get to that stage of performance maturity, these strategies may be used:

1. Give students the graphic organizer forms to fill-in.

2. Show students examples of well-done, completed graphic organizers and graphic organizers with obvious flaws, and have students work in small groups to critique the graphic organizers and fix the flaws.

3. Allow students to pick the format for the graphic organizer that they will use for a particular performance task from a poster collection of graphic organizers displayed in the classroom.

4. Allow students to create their own formats for graphic organizers.

5. Do not even mention graphic organizers because students should be using these strategies independently.

THINKING SKILL VERBS AND THEIR GRAPHIC ORGANIZERS

VERB   Each Diagram is a Graphic Organizer Which Processes Information According to the Verb

A. **Sequence** (linear)

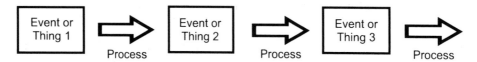

B. **Sequence** (cycle)

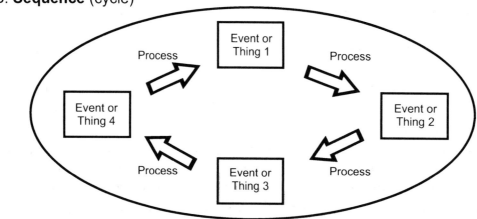

C. **Compare and Contrast**

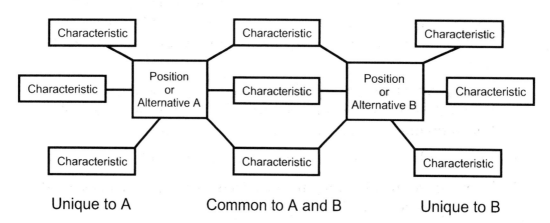

D. **Find/Describe Cause(s) and Effects(s)**

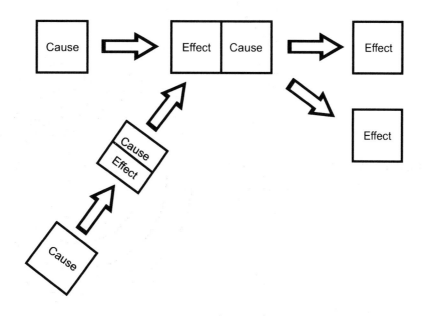

E. **Categorize** (in this case, a dichotomous key)

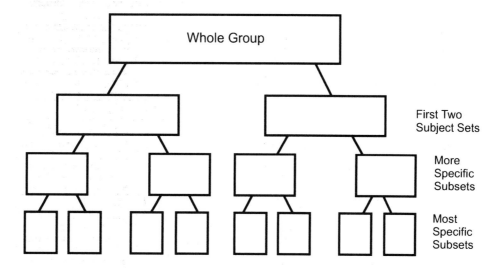

F. Make an Analogy For

G. Describe General To Specific

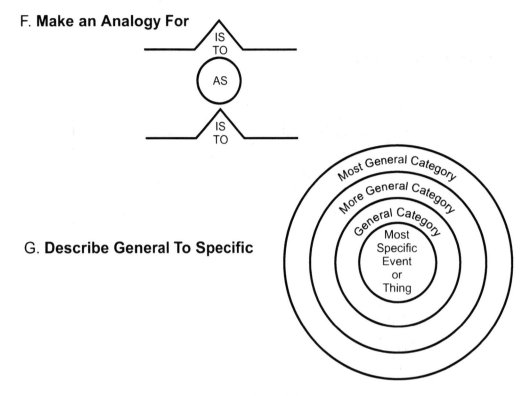

H. Generalize to State Thesis or Big Idea

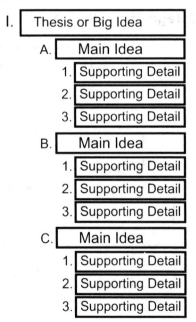

I. **Predict With Evidence**

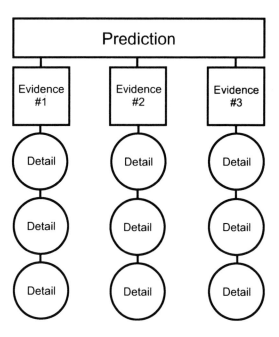

J. **Infer With Support**

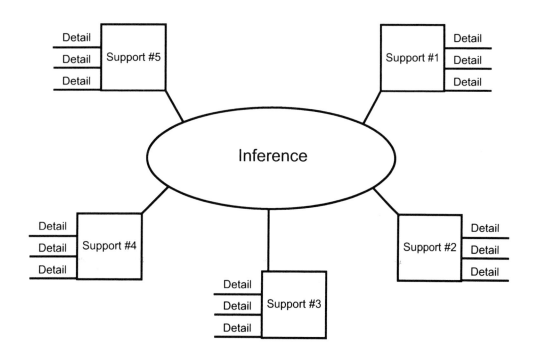

APPENDIX C

A COLLECTION OF PERFORMANCE PROFILES FOR VARIOUS FORMATS OF STUDENT WORK

The Performance Profiles in this appendix are to be used in three ways: First, they are menus of ideas for items of assessment lists. Second, they provide a framework for teachers to have conversations about the strengths and weaknesses of student performance. And third, they can be used to describe the level of performance (Expert, Proficient, Novice, Beginning) of a student.

PERFORMANCE PROFILES AS MENUS OF IDEAS FOR ASSESSMENT LISTS

This collection of Performance Profiles helps teachers create performance tasks tailored to specific performance tasks and to the specific performance maturity of their students. For example, the profile for and oral presentation is longer than any assessment list that would actually be used in the classroom. This list of skills for an oral presentation is intended to be a menu of ideas for the teacher. The wording of an assessment list changes depending on the topic of that presentation. The number of items and their specificity changes depending on the performance maturity of the students. Remember that the purpose of the assessment is to get students to pay as much attention as possible to the quality of their work.

After students have experience with using assessment lists that you make, let them be more involved in making the lists. You can display these dimensions in the classroom to serve as menus of ideas for students. Some strategies to follow to coach students to be more performance-mature learners are:

1. Give students short, very specific assessment lists.

2. Have students work in small groups to use these simple assessment lists to critique samples of student work that you provide.

3. Gradually make the assessment lists more demanding.

4. Have the class help you make an assessment list. Shape the items on the list with the aid of the entire class.

5. Have the students work in small groups to create the assessment list. Use the work of all the groups to compile one assessment list that all students in the class will use.

6. Have each student work alone to create assessment lists. Use these individually created lists to compile one assessment list that all the students in the class will use.

7. Have each student work alone to create an assessment list. When a student's list meets your standards, have the student use that assessment list for his or her work.

8. Have the students work without an assessment list. Each student should be using the assessment list that is in his or her mind.

PERFORMANCE PROFILES AS FRAMEWORKS FOR CONVERSATIONS AMONG TEACHERS

Consider the Performance Profile for a multimedia presentation. Teachers can use this list of skills to identify the overall strengths and weaknesses of a class, grade level, or several grade levels of students in their performance of planning and creating a multimedia presentation on a science topic. Subsequent instruction, performance tasks, and assessment lists can be designed to address what students need to learn to improve in their performance in planning and creating multimedia presentations. The analytical nature of these lists allows teachers to fine-tune their materials and work.

PERFORMANCE PROFILES AS TOOLS TO DESCRIBE AND DOCUMENT THE PROFICIENCY LEVEL OF A STUDENT'S PERFORMANCE

Any of these Performance Profiles can also be viewed as an inventory of the overall competency level of a student. The performance level (Expert, Proficient, Novice, or Beginning) of an individual student can be assessed. For example, the goal may be for all students to reach the Proficient level by the end of eighth grade. The assessment permits individual attention to students who are making insufficient progress toward that goal.

INDEX TO PERFORMANCE PROFILES

This page is intentionally blank.

PERFORMANCE PROFILE FOR A DATA CHART

Student Name: _____ Grade Level: _____

Date of Assessment: _____ Assessor: _____

Skill	Level of Proficiency			
	Expert	*Proficient*	*Novice*	*Beginning*
1. Explains the reason for making the data chart.	_____	_____	_____	_____
2. Selects or creates a format for the data chart appropriate to the task.	_____	_____	_____	_____
3. Data is organized according to the categories relevant to the task.	_____	_____	_____	_____
4. Titles and labels are used to describe all elements of the data chart.	_____	_____	_____	_____
5. Units of measurement are accurate and clearly marked.	_____	_____	_____	_____
6. Appropriate statistical procedures are used and included in the data chart according to the requirements of the task.	_____	_____	_____	_____
7. Computations are accurate.	_____	_____	_____	_____
8. The work is neat and presentable.	_____	_____	_____	_____

OVERALL LEVEL OF PROFICIENCY

_____ Expert   _____ Proficient   _____ Novice   _____ Beginning

GOALS FOR IMPROVEMENT

PERFORMANCE PROFILE FOR
TECHNICAL, INFORMATIONAL, AND EXPOSITORY WRITING

Student Name: _____   Grade Level: _____

Date of Assessment: _____   Assessor: _____

Skill	*Level of Proficiency*			
	Expert	*Proficient*	*Novice*	*Beginning*

PREWRITING

1. The student restates the topic for the assignment in his or her own words and understands the format for the final written product, the audience for that writing, and the purpose the writing is to have for that audience.

2. The verb(s) that direct the type(s) of information processing to be accomplished through the graphic organizer(s) is/are identified and used. (For example, the "driving verb" may be sequence, compare, generalize, infer, predict, relate cause and effect. Graphic organizers are selected with formats to fit the processing called for by the verbs.)

3. Graphic organizer(s) is/are used to plan the structure and content of the writing. (The use of the graphic organizer shows that the student processed information rather than only copying it from a source.)

4. Information is from valid resources. Identify information that may be inaccurate and/or biased.

5. All information is accurate and is used in sufficient quantity to support the main ideas.

Skill	*Level of Proficiency*			
	Expert	*Proficient*	*Novice*	*Beginning*
6. Information from all required sources is used.	____	____	____	____
7. Sources of information are properly identified in a bibliography or work cited list.	____	____	____	____

FIRST DRAFT WRITING

8. The thesis is clear, concise, and accurate according to its connection to the assignment.	____	____	____	____
9. The introduction arouses interest, narrows and focuses the topic, and states the thesis clearly.	____	____	____	____
10. Sufficient, clear, concise, and accurate main ideas develop the thesis.	____	____	____	____
11. Main ideas are sequenced best to support the thesis.	____	____	____	____
12. Each paragraph has a clear topic sentence.	____	____	____	____
13. Sufficient, specific, and accurate facts support each main idea.	____	____	____	____
14. Supporting details are sequenced to best develop the main idea.	____	____	____	____
15. Transition words or phrases come at the beginning of paragraphs.	____	____	____	____
16. The sequence of main ideas and supporting details, the use of transition words and phrases, and the use of a variety of sentence structures (simple, compound, and complex) provides a smooth flow to the writing.	____	____	____	____
17. The writing stays on topic.	____	____	____	____
18. Direct quotes and paraphrases are properly identified in parenthetical notations according to M.L.A. standards.	____	____	____	____

Skill	*Level of Proficiency*			
	Expert	*Proficient*	*Novice*	*Beginning*
19. Connections between main ideas and contextual evidence is explained. Explanations of quoted materials are twice as long as the quote itself.	____	____	____	____
20. Each paragraph uses vocabulary that is accurate according to the topic and appropriate to the audience for the final product.	____	____	____	____
21. Each paragraph has a closing sentence.	____	____	____	____
22. The conclusion to the paper is made according to the specific format of the product assigned.	____	____	____	____
23. Visuals are used to enhance the reader's understanding of the material.	____	____	____	____
24. Overall the paper is clear and effective; it accomplishes its purpose with its audience.	____	____	____	____
25. Overall the paper shows a deep understanding of the thesis rather than a superficial treatment of information.	____	____	____	____

EDITING

26. There should be evidence of:				
a. Effective word choice	____	____	____	____
b. Combining simple sentences	____	____	____	____
c. Periodic order	____	____	____	____
d. Parallel structure	____	____	____	____
e. Effective subordination/coordination	____	____	____	____

Skill	Level of Proficiency			
	Expert	Proficient	Novice	Beginning
f. Transition words are used to help tie the overall writing together. The selection and placement of transition words and/or phrases are made according to the needs of the paper.	____	____	____	____
g. Punctuation including comma rules, end punctuation, apostrophe, quotation marks, colon, and semicolon	____	____	____	____
h. Capitalization	____	____	____	____
i. Spelling	____	____	____	____
j. Usage	____	____	____	____
k. All elements of format are followed for the written product assigned.	____	____	____	____

REVISING

	Expert	Proficient	Novice	Beginning
27. The following elements are true of this writing:	____	____	____	____
a. Each paragraph develops an important topic accurately, thoroughly, precisely, and concisely.	____	____	____	____
b. All information is on the topic with no "side trips."	____	____	____	____
c. Information is presented without unnecessary redundancy.	____	____	____	____

OVERALL LEVEL OF PROFICIENCY

____ Expert   ____ Proficient   ____ Novice   ____ Beginning

GOALS FOR IMPROVEMENT

PERFORMANCE PROFILE FOR A BAR OR LINE GRAPH

Student Name: _____   Grade Level: _____

Date of Assessment: _____   Assessor: _____

Skill	*Level of Proficiency*			
	Expert	*Proficient*	*Novice*	*Beginning*
1. Explains the reason for making the graph.	_____	_____	_____	_____
2. Explains who the audience is for the graph and what the graph is intended to accomplish for that audience.	_____	_____	_____	_____
3. Selects or creates the type of a graph (a bar graph or a line graph) that is appropriate for the data and also for the audience.	_____	_____	_____	_____
4. Labels and titles are concise and accurate.	_____	_____	_____	_____
5. The scale for each axis is appropriate for the range of data to be plotted on that axis.	_____	_____	_____	_____
6. The scales are chosen so that the data are presented in an objective manner.	_____	_____	_____	_____
7. The scale for each axis is accurate and the units of measurement are shown.	_____	_____	_____	_____
8. The whole space of the graph is well used.	_____	_____	_____	_____
9. The data are plotted accurately.	_____	_____	_____	_____
10. Actual data and extrapolations from that data are kept separate on the graph.	_____	_____	_____	_____
11. Color, texture, symbols, and other graphic strategies are used to make the graph easy to understand.	_____	_____	_____	_____

Skill	*Level of Proficiency*			
	Expert	*Proficient*	*Novice*	*Beginning*
12. The key is clear and complete.	_____	_____	_____	_____
13. The work is neat and presentable.	_____	_____	_____	_____
14. Mechanics of English are accurate.	_____	_____	_____	_____

OVERALL LEVEL OF PROFICIENCY

_____ Expert   _____ Proficient   _____ Novice   _____ Beginning

GOALS FOR IMPROVEMENT

PERFORMANCE PROFILE FOR AN INVENTION

Student Name: _____   Grade Level: _____

Date of Assessment: _____   Assessor: _____

Skill	*Level of Proficiency*			
	Expert	*Proficient*	*Novice*	*Beginning*
1. Explains the reason for making the invention. That is, the student defines the problem to be solved or the human need to be met.	_____	_____	_____	_____
2. Identifies the audience for the invention. That is, the student defines the customer for or the intended user of the invention.	_____	_____	_____	_____
3. Lists the specifications that the invention must meet. These specifications can include: Function(s) to Accomplish Construction Materials to be Used Cost Durability Environmental Impact Aesthetics	_____	_____	_____	_____
4. Makes a list of the science principles behind the invention.	_____	_____	_____	_____
5. Makes sketches from at least two perspectives.	_____	_____	_____	_____
6. Sketches are made to scale.	_____	_____	_____	_____
7. Labels are used to describe how the plan shows the structures and their function.	_____	_____	_____	_____
8. Labels are used to describe the materials to be used.	_____	_____	_____	_____
9. Writes an explanation of the scientific principles that are central to this invention.	_____	_____	_____	_____
10. Uses color, textures, and other graphic devices are to make the plan easier to understand.	_____	_____	_____	_____

Skill	Level of Proficiency			
	Expert	Proficient	Novice	Beginning
11. The invention works.	_____	_____	_____	_____
12. The invention works reliably.	_____	_____	_____	_____
13. The invention meets all design specifications.	_____	_____	_____	_____
14. The invention is safe.	_____	_____	_____	_____

OVERALL LEVEL OF PROFICIENCY

_____ Expert   _____ Proficient   _____ Novice   _____ Beginning

GOALS FOR IMPROVEMENT

PERFORMANCE PROFILE FOR
MAKING SCIENTIFIC OBSERVATIONS

Student Name: _____   Grade Level: _____

Date of Assessment: _____   Assessor: _____

Skill	*Level of Proficiency*			
	Expert	*Proficient*	*Novice*	*Beginning*
1. Makes many observations.	_____	_____	_____	_____
2. Makes detailed observations.	_____	_____	_____	_____
3. Makes observations from more than one perspective.	_____	_____	_____	_____
4. Uses drawings and sketches.	_____	_____	_____	_____
5. Makes quantitative observations accurately.	_____	_____	_____	_____
6. Uses the metric system accurately and appropriately.	_____	_____	_____	_____
7. Uses scientific notation accurately and appropriately.	_____	_____	_____	_____
8. Uses other standard quantitative systems accurately and appropriately.	_____	_____	_____	_____
9. Uses appropriate units.	_____	_____	_____	_____
10. Uses appropriate number of significant figures.	_____	_____	_____	_____
11. Makes qualitative observations when appropriate (i.e., when quantitative systems are not available).	_____	_____	_____	_____
12. Uses descriptive language to define qualitative observations.	_____	_____	_____	_____
13. Invents qualitative scales when appropriate.	_____	_____	_____	_____
14. Organizes observations into charts, tables, and graphs.	_____	_____	_____	_____
15. Separates inferences and extrapolations from actual observations.	_____	_____	_____	_____

Skill	*Level of Proficiency*			
	Expert	*Proficient*	*Novice*	*Beginning*
16. Organizes the observations in categories according to the purpose(s) for the observations.	_____	_____	_____	_____
17. Labels all data.	_____	_____	_____	_____
18. Observation logs are neat and organized.	_____	_____	_____	_____
19. Observation logs have correct heading, titles, and other information.	_____	_____	_____	_____

OVERALL LEVEL OF PROFICIENCY

_____ Expert   _____ Proficient   _____ Novice   _____ Beginning

GOALS FOR IMPROVEMENT

PERFORMANCE PROFILE FOR A MAP

Student Name: _____ Grade Level: _____

Date of Assessment: _____ Assessor: _____

Skill	*Level of Proficiency*			
	Expert	*Proficient*	*Novice*	*Beginning*
1. Explains the reason for making the map.	_____	_____	_____	_____
2. Identifies the audience for the map.	_____	_____	_____	_____
3. Identifies the format for the map.	_____	_____	_____	_____
4. Identifies the criteria to be used to judge the quality of the map.	_____	_____	_____	_____
5. Finds and uses appropriate information.	_____	_____	_____	_____
6. Makes a rough sketch of the map and annotates how the map shows what it intends to show.	_____	_____	_____	_____
7. Uses an appropriate scale.	_____	_____	_____	_____
8. Geography is represented accurately.	_____	_____	_____	_____
9. Physical, economic, social, political, or other factors are represented accurately and clearly.	_____	_____	_____	_____
10. Color, textures, and other graphics are used to provide the information needed and make the map easy to understand.	_____	_____	_____	_____
11. Annotations and labels are used to make the map easy to understand.	_____	_____	_____	_____
12. A key provides explanation of relevant information.	_____	_____	_____	_____
13. The map is neat and presentable.	_____	_____	_____	_____

OVERALL LEVEL OF PROFICIENCY

_____ Expert   _____ Proficient   _____ Novice   _____ Beginning

GOALS FOR IMPROVEMENT

PERFORMANCE PROFILE FOR A
SCIENCE MODEL

Student Name: _____ Grade Level: _____

Date of Assessment: _____ Assessor: _____

Skill	*Level of Proficiency*			
	Expert	*Proficient*	*Novice*	*Beginning*
1. Explains the reason for making the model.	_____	_____	_____	_____
2. Identifies the audience for the model.	_____	_____	_____	_____
3. Identifies the format for the model.	_____	_____	_____	_____
4. Identifies the criteria to be used to judge the quality of the model.	_____	_____	_____	_____
5. Makes a list of what science the model is intended to show.	_____	_____	_____	_____
6. Makes a sketch of the model from at least two perspectives.	_____	_____	_____	_____
7. Labels and annotates the sketch of the model to explain how the science content will be shown.	_____	_____	_____	_____
8. The model clearly shows the elements of the real thing that are intended to present the science content of the task.	_____	_____	_____	_____
9. Color, labels, and other techniques are used to direct the viewer to the appropriate parts of the model.	_____	_____	_____	_____
10. A written explanation of what the model shows accompanies the model.	_____	_____	_____	_____
11. The most important ways in which the model is an INACCURATE representation of the real thing are listed.	_____	_____	_____	_____

Skill	*Level of Proficiency*			
	Expert	*Proficient*	*Novice*	*Beginning*
12. The model is durable and safe.	_____	_____	_____	_____
13. The model shows excellent craftsmanship.	_____	_____	_____	_____

OVERALL LEVEL OF PROFICIENCY

_____ Expert   _____ Proficient   _____ Novice   _____ Beginning

GOALS FOR IMPROVEMENT

PERFORMANCE PROFILE FOR A
MULTIMEDIA PRESENTATION

Student Name: _____   Grade Level: _____

Date of Assessment: _____   Assessor: _____

Skill	Level of Proficiency			
	Expert	Proficient	Novice	Beginning

UNDERSTANDS THE TASK

1. Shows understanding of the task for which the multimedia presentation is necessary.

2. Shows understanding of the audience for the final product and how to tailor the final product to that audience.

3. Shows understanding of the criteria to be used to assess the quality of the final product.

PLANS THE WORK (A Series of Screens)

Note: If research is part of this task, the student carries out the research according to the skills described in the Learning Resources and Information Technology framework.

4. Brainstorms ideas for the presentation.

5. Sketches each screen. Sketches include graphics and location of text.

6. Links in the graphics and the text to other screens are made. Special effects to be used are noted.

7. Drafts the text fields for each screen. Words which will become links to other screens are identified.

OBTAINS MULTIMEDIA MATERIAL FOR THE PRESENTATION

8. Finds and adds graphics copied from clip art.

9. Creates and adds graphics using graphic tools.

Skill	*Level of Proficiency*			
	Expert	*Proficient*	*Novice*	*Beginning*
10. Finds/makes and adds photos from a variety of sources.	____	____	____	____
11. Finds and adds scanned images.	____	____	____	____
12. Adds images from a digital camera.	____	____	____	____
13. Creates and adds animation.	____	____	____	____
14. Finds/makes and adds video segments.	____	____	____	____
15. Finds and adds dialogue and/or sound effects including prerecorded music.	____	____	____	____
16. Adds button/menu so the viewer can navigate among the screens.	____	____	____	____

THE MULTIMEDIA PRESENTATION

	Expert	*Proficient*	*Novice*	*Beginning*
17. The graphics and text on each card are accurate and clear.	____	____	____	____
18. Transition effects are used between cards.	____	____	____	____
19. Transition effects enhance the content of the stack and are appropriate and effective.	____	____	____	____
20. There is a logical, coherent progression from one card to the next.	____	____	____	____
21. Background colors and textures enhance the content and do not detract from the message.	____	____	____	____
22. Text color complements the background making the card easy to read.	____	____	____	____
23. Text size and style are appropriate.	____	____	____	____
24. Scroll bars are removed when possible.	____	____	____	____
25. Animation is used effectively and appropriately.	____	____	____	____

Skill	Level of Proficiency			
	Expert	Proficient	Novice	Beginning
26. Sound adds to the meaning and enhances understanding of the card.	_____	_____	_____	_____
27. All information is accurate.	_____	_____	_____	_____
28. The presentation is appropriate to the audience for which it is intended.	_____	_____	_____	_____
29. The whole presentation is focused on the topic.	_____	_____	_____	_____
30. The whole stack flows smoothly.	_____	_____	_____	_____
31. There are no spelling errors.	_____	_____	_____	_____
32. There are no errors of English mechanics.	_____	_____	_____	_____

WORK HABITS

	Expert	Proficient	Novice	Beginning
33. Follows directions.	_____	_____	_____	_____
34. Works independently when appropriate.	_____	_____	_____	_____
35. Works collaboratively when appropriate.	_____	_____	_____	_____
36. Is organized.	_____	_____	_____	_____
37. Is persistent.	_____	_____	_____	_____
38. Manages time.	_____	_____	_____	_____

OVERALL LEVEL OF PROFICIENCY

_____ Expert   _____ Proficient   _____ Novice   _____ Beginning

GOALS FOR IMPROVEMENT

PERFORMANCE PROFILE FOR
WRITING A NEWSPAPER ARTICLE

Student Name: _____   Grade Level: _____

Date of Assessment: _____   Assessor: _____

Skill	*Level of Proficiency*			
	Expert	*Proficient*	*Novice*	*Beginning*
1. The writing, either assigned or selected, is on the topic.	_____	_____	_____	_____
2. The big idea or thesis of the writing is clear.	_____	_____	_____	_____
3. The Who, What, When, Where, Why, and How are addressed.	_____	_____	_____	_____
4. There are at least three accurate and appropriate main ideas.	_____	_____	_____	_____
5. Each main idea has at least three accurate and appropriate supporting details.	_____	_____	_____	_____
6. The sequence of main ideas and supporting details for those main ideas presents the overall theme effectively.	_____	_____	_____	_____
7. The information is from sources beyond the text.	_____	_____	_____	_____
8. Quotes add interest.	_____	_____	_____	_____
9. Sources of information are cited.	_____	_____	_____	_____
10. Research notes indicate how the quality of the information source and the information gathered were determined.	_____	_____	_____	_____
11. Topic-specific vocabulary is used correctly and with consideration of the audience for this writing.	_____	_____	_____	_____

Skill	*Level of Proficiency*			
	Expert	*Proficient*	*Novice*	*Beginning*
12. Thinking skills appropriate to the topic are evident. (Examples of thinking skills that direct the organization of the writing include: compare/contrast, cause/effect, sequence, making and supporting an inference, and predicting with evidence.)	____	____	____	____
13. The writing stays on topic.	____	____	____	____
14. The transitions between ideas are smooth. Words to signal transition are used.	____	____	____	____
15. Graphs, charts, or illustrations may be used to support the writing.	____	____	____	____
16. The title grabs the reader's attention.	____	____	____	____
17. The work is neat and presentable.	____	____	____	____
18. The mechanics of English are correct.	____	____	____	____
19. The work is completed on time.	____	____	____	____

OVERALL LEVEL OF PROFICIENCY

____ Expert   ____ Proficient   ____ Novice   ____ Beginning

GOALS FOR IMPROVEMENT

PERFORMANCE PROFILE FOR AN ORAL PRESENTATION

Student Name: _____   Grade Level: _____

Date of Assessment: _____   Assessor: _____

Skill	*Level of Proficiency*			
	Expert	Proficient	Novice	Beginning

UNDERSTANDING THE ASSIGNMENT

	Expert	Proficient	Novice	Beginning
1. Explains the reason for the oral presentation.	____	____	____	____
2. Identifies the audience for the presentation.	____	____	____	____
3. Identifies the format for the oral presentation.	____	____	____	____
4. Identifies the criteria to be used to judge the quality of the oral presentation.	____	____	____	____

PLANNING THE ORAL PRESENTATION

	Expert	Proficient	Novice	Beginning
5. Lists research questions that will direct the search for information for the oral presentation.	____	____	____	____
6. Finds and uses appropriate information.	____	____	____	____
7. Organizes information from research on note cards or into a graphic organizer in preparation for writing the outline or the script for the oral presentation.	____	____	____	____

THE CONTENT OF THE ORAL PRESENTATION

	Expert	Proficient	Novice	Beginning
8. The thesis or main idea is clear and appropriate to the task.	____	____	____	____
9. The content is accurate.	____	____	____	____
10. The examples given are sufficient and appropriate to both audience and topic.	____	____	____	____

Skill	Level of Proficiency			
	Expert	Proficient	Novice	Beginning
11. Thinking skills are used which are appropriate to the task and help the audience understand the content of the presentation.	____	____	____	____
12. The organization shows a clear beginning, middle, and ending.	____	____	____	____
13. The vocabulary is appropriate to the topic and to the audience.	____	____	____	____

SUPPORTING GRAPHS AND/OR PROPS

Skill	Expert	Proficient	Novice	Beginning
14. The presentation has more impact because of the graphics (including electronic or multimedia) and/or props used.	____	____	____	____
15. The audience can easily see the graphics and/or props used.	____	____	____	____

PRESENTATION STRATEGIES

Skill	Expert	Proficient	Novice	Beginning
16. The speaker provides an "attention-getting" introduction appropriate to the task and to the audience.	____	____	____	____
17. The audience is asked to think about what is being said and is given the time to think.	____	____	____	____
18. The audience is actively involved.	____	____	____	____
19. Humor is used appropriately.	____	____	____	____
20. The speaker takes the perspective of the audience.	____	____	____	____
21. The speaker tells the audience what he or she is going to say, says it, and highlights what was said.	____	____	____	____
22. The rate of speech and inflections used help the audience understand what is being said.	____	____	____	____
23. Eye contact is made with the entire audience.	____	____	____	____

Skill	Level of Proficiency			
	Expert	Proficient	Novice	Beginning
24. Body language adds to the presentation.	_____	_____	_____	_____
25. The speaker sticks to the time allotted.	_____	_____	_____	_____
26. The speaker uses a closing that is memorable.	_____	_____	_____	_____

PRESENTATION MECHANICS

	Expert	Proficient	Novice	Beginning
27. The voice is clear and loud enough to be heard by everyone in the audience.	_____	_____	_____	_____
28. Grammar and diction are correct.	_____	_____	_____	_____
29. Posture is correct.	_____	_____	_____	_____
30. The use of note cards, graphics, technology, and/or props are handled smoothly so that the audience hardly notices.	_____	_____	_____	_____
31. The speaker is dressed appropriately.	_____	_____	_____	_____
32. The speaker has a neat appearance.	_____	_____	_____	_____

OVERALL LEVEL OF PROFICIENCY

_____ Expert   _____ Proficient   _____ Novice   _____ Beginning

GOALS FOR IMPROVEMENT

PERFORMANCE PROFILE FOR A POSTER

Student Name: _____   Grade Level: _____

Date of Assessment: _____   Assessor: _____

Skill	*Level of Proficiency*			
	Expert	*Proficient*	*Novice*	*Beginning*
1. Explains the reason for making the poster.	_____	_____	_____	_____
2. Identifies the audience for the poster.	_____	_____	_____	_____
3. Identifies the format for the poster.	_____	_____	_____	_____
4. Identifies the criteria to be used to judge the quality of the poster.	_____	_____	_____	_____
5. Finds and uses appropriate information.	_____	_____	_____	_____
6. Makes a rough sketch of the poster and annotates how the poster shows what it is intended to show.	_____	_____	_____	_____
7. The scientific principle is shown accurately.	_____	_____	_____	_____
8. The most important elements of the scientific principle for this poster stand out clearly.	_____	_____	_____	_____
9. Details add clarity and do not obstruct the main point being displayed.	_____	_____	_____	_____
10. Color, textures, and other graphics are used to provide the information needed and make the poster easy to understand.	_____	_____	_____	_____
11. Annotations and labels are used to make the poster easy to understand.	_____	_____	_____	_____

Skill	Level of Proficiency			
	Expert	Proficient	Novice	Beginning
12. In ten seconds, the audience can understand what the poster is intending to communicate.	_____	_____	_____	_____
13. The poster is neat and presentable.	_____	_____	_____	_____

OVERALL LEVEL OF PROFICIENCY

_____ Expert   _____ Proficient   _____ Novice   _____ Beginning

GOALS FOR IMPROVEMENT

PERFORMANCE PROFILE FOR
RESEARCH SKILLS

Student Name: _____ Grade Level: _____

Date of Assessment: _____ Assessor: _____

Skill	*Level of Proficiency*			
	Expert	Proficient	Novice	Beginning

DEFINING INFORMATION NEEDS

1. Shows understanding of the task for which research is necessary.	_____	_____	_____	_____
2. Shows understanding of the audience for the final product and how to tailor the final product to that audience.	_____	_____	_____	_____
3. Shows understanding of the criteria to be used in assessment of the quality of the final product.	_____	_____	_____	_____

INFORMATION STRATEGIES

4. States the essential question or thesis for the research topic.	_____	_____	_____	_____
5. Identifies subtopics or questions to direct the research.	_____	_____	_____	_____
6. Clarifies what is already known relevant to the specific research questions.	_____	_____	_____	_____
7. Clarifies the criteria used to judge the quality, type, and quantity of information sources required for the research.	_____	_____	_____	_____
8. Develops a time and task management plan for the research and development of the final product.	_____	_____	_____	_____

INFORMATION SYSTEMS

9. Identifies facilities and resources available.	_____	_____	_____	_____
10. Understands the issues of schedules, hours of availability, and scarce resources.	_____	_____	_____	_____

Skill	*Level of Proficiency*			
	Expert	*Proficient*	*Novice*	*Beginning*
11. Has the skills to access the information sources selected.	_____	_____	_____	_____

INFORMATION PROCESSING

12. Judges the suitability of the information source according to the criteria already established.	_____	_____	_____	_____
13. Gets suitable information from print resources.	_____	_____	_____	_____
14. Gets suitable information from electronic resources.	_____	_____	_____	_____
15. Gets information from direct experience including observations and interviews.	_____	_____	_____	_____
16. Gets information from the proper number and types of sources.	_____	_____	_____	_____
17. Summarizes information using outlines, graphic organizers, note cards, or other strategies.	_____	_____	_____	_____

RESPONSIBLE INFORMATION USE

18. Properly identifies quotes.	_____	_____	_____	_____
19. Properly identifies paraphrases.	_____	_____	_____	_____
20. Uses complete and correct bibliographic procedures.	_____	_____	_____	_____

WORK HABITS

21. Follows directions.	_____	_____	_____	_____
22. Manages time.	_____	_____	_____	_____
23. Is persistent.	_____	_____	_____	_____
24. Is organized.	_____	_____	_____	_____
25. Works independently when appropriate.	_____	_____	_____	_____
26. Works collaboratively when appropriate.	_____	_____	_____	_____
27. Uses feedback to improve work.	_____	_____	_____	_____

Skill	*Level of Proficiency*			
	Expert	*Proficient*	*Novice*	*Beginning*

APPLICATION

28. The student incorporates the information from this research in the final product for the task. See the Assessment of Word Processing, Assessment of Multimedia Projects, or other forms for final products.

OVERALL LEVEL OF PROFICIENCY

_____ Expert   _____ Proficient   _____ Novice   _____ Beginning

GOALS FOR IMPROVEMENT

PERFORMANCE PROFILE FOR A
SCIENTIFIC DRAWING

Student Name: _____ Grade Level: _____

Date of Assessment: _____ Assessor: _____

Skill	*Level of Proficiency*			
	Expert	*Proficient*	*Novice*	*Beginning*
1. Explains the reason for making the drawing.	_____	_____	_____	_____
2. Identifies the audience for the drawing.	_____	_____	_____	_____
3. Identifies the format for the drawing.	_____	_____	_____	_____
4. Identifies the criteria to be used to judge the quality of the drawing.	_____	_____	_____	_____
5. Finds and uses appropriate information.	_____	_____	_____	_____
6. Makes a rough sketch of the drawing and annotates how the drawing shows what it intends to show.	_____	_____	_____	_____
7. Plans how to show more than one perspective of what is drawn.	_____	_____	_____	_____
8. Is accurate.	_____	_____	_____	_____
9. Uses an appropriate scale.	_____	_____	_____	_____
10. Uses at least two perspectives.	_____	_____	_____	_____
11. Shows details according to the purpose of the drawing.	_____	_____	_____	_____
12. Color, textures, and other graphics are used to provide the information needed and make the drawing easy to understand.	_____	_____	_____	_____
13. Annotations and/or labels are used to make the drawing easy to understand.	_____	_____	_____	_____

Skill	Level of Proficiency			
	Expert	Proficient	Novice	Beginning
14. A key provides explanation of relevant information.	_____	_____	_____	_____
15. The drawing is neat and presentable.	_____	_____	_____	_____

OVERALL LEVEL OF PROFICIENCY

_____ Expert   _____ Proficient   _____ Novice   _____ Beginning

GOALS FOR IMPROVEMENT

PERFORMANCE PROFILE FOR A SCIENCE SKIT

Student Name: _____ Grade Level: _____

Date of Assessment: _____ Assessor: _____

Skill	*Level of Proficiency*			
	Expert	*Proficient*	*Novice*	*Beginning*
1. Explains the reason for the skit.	_____	_____	_____	_____
2. Identifies the audience for the skit.	_____	_____	_____	_____
3. Identifies the criteria to be used in judging the quality of the skit.	_____	_____	_____	_____
4. Makes a list of what science the skit is intended to demonstrate.	_____	_____	_____	_____
5. Plans for any special characters to have parts in the skit.	_____	_____	_____	_____
6. Makes a storyboard to show the sequence of events in the skit.	_____	_____	_____	_____
7. Annotates the storyboard to show any dialogue for the part of the skit.	_____	_____	_____	_____
8. Plans for props and costumes if they are to be used.	_____	_____	_____	_____
9. The thesis or main idea is clear and appropriate to the task.	_____	_____	_____	_____
10. The sequence of events in the skit shows the science intended.	_____	_____	_____	_____
11. The science information is on topic and accurate.	_____	_____	_____	_____
12. The organization shows a clear beginning, middle, and ending, and support the science content being presented.	_____	_____	_____	_____
13. The vocabulary in the dialogue is appropriate to the topic and to the audience.	_____	_____	_____	_____

	Skill	*Expert*	*Proficient*	*Novice*	*Beginning*
			Level of Proficiency		
14.	The skit provides an "attention-getting" introduction appropriate to the task and to the audience.	____	____	____	____
15.	Actions are "larger than life" to emphasize the science content.	____	____	____	____
16.	Characterization through voice and/or costume and/or props helps to present the science content.	____	____	____	____
17.	The audience may be actively involved.	____	____	____	____
18.	Humor is used appropriately.	____	____	____	____
19.	The skit has a memorable ending.	____	____	____	____
20.	The dialogue is clear and loud enough to be heard by everyone in the audience.	____	____	____	____
21.	Grammar and diction are correct according to the role of the speaker in the skit.	____	____	____	____
22.	Characterization through the use of voice makes the science content easier to understand.	____	____	____	____

OVERALL LEVEL OF PROFICIENCY

_____ Expert   _____ Proficient   _____ Novice   _____ Beginning

GOALS FOR IMPROVEMENT

PERFORMANCE PROFILE FOR A
WRITTEN SUMMARY OF A BAR OR LINE GRAPH

Student Name: _____   Grade Level: _____

Date of Assessment: _____   Assessor: _____

Skill	*Level of Proficiency*			
	Expert	*Proficient*	*Novice*	*Beginning*
1. Explains the reason for making the written summary of the graph.	_____	_____	_____	_____
2. Explains who the audience is for the written summary and what the written summary is intended to accomplish for that audience.	_____	_____	_____	_____
3. Uses a concept map graphic organizer to plan the main ideas and supporting details for the written summary.	_____	_____	_____	_____
4. The title presents the overall theme of the graph.	_____	_____	_____	_____
5. Each main idea of what the graph actually shows is presented.	_____	_____	_____	_____
6. Each main idea is supported by data from the graph.	_____	_____	_____	_____
7. Extrapolations and predictions, if made, are kept separate from the description of what the graph actually shows.	_____	_____	_____	_____
8. The summary is organized.	_____	_____	_____	_____
9. The summary uses vocabulary relevant to what the graph is about and appropriate for the audience for which this graph is intended.				
10. The work is neat and presentable.				
11. Mechanics of English are accurate.	_____	_____	_____	_____

OVERALL LEVEL OF PROFICIENCY

_____ Expert   _____ Proficient   _____ Novice   _____ Beginning

GOALS FOR IMPROVEMENT